BABYLOVE

CHOOSING MOTHERHOOD

After a Lifetime of Ambivalence

Rebecca Walker

RIVERHEAD BOOKS

a member of Penguin Group (USA) Inc.

New York

2007

RIVERHEAD BOOKS
Published by the Penguin Group
Penguin Group (USA) Inc., 375 Hudson Street, New York, New York 10014, USA
• Penguin Group (Canada), 90 Eglinton Avenue East, Suite 700, Toronto, Ontario
M4P 2Y3, Canada (a division of Pearson Penguin Canada Inc.) • Penguin Books
Ltd, 80 Strand, London WC2R 0RL, England • Penguin Ireland, 25 St Stephen's
Green, Dublin 2, Ireland (a division of Penguin Books Ltd) • Penguin Group
(Australia), 250 Camberwell Road, Camberwell, Victoria 3124, Australia
(a division of Pearson Australia Group Pty Ltd) • Penguin Books India Pvt Ltd,
11 Community Centre, Panchsheel Park, New Delhi–110 017, India
• Penguin Group (NZ), 67 Apollo Drive, Mairangi Bay, Auckland 1311,
New Zealand (a division of Pearson New Zealand Ltd) • Penguin Books
(South Africa) (Pty) Ltd, 24 Sturdee Avenue, Rosebank,
Johannesburg 2196, South Africa

Penguin Books Ltd, Registered Offices:
80 Strand, London WC2R 0RL, England

Passages on pages 10, 75, and 138 are quoted from the Baby
Centre website (www.babycentre.co.uk).

Library of Congress Cataloging-in-Publication Data

Walker, Rebecca, date.
Baby love : choosing motherhood after
a lifetime of ambivalence / Rebecca Walker.
p.   cm.
ISBN 978-1-59448-943-3
1. Walker, Rebecca.   2. Pregnant women—United States— Biography.
3. Pregnancy—Psychological aspects.   4. Motherhood— Psychological
aspects.   5. Ambivalence.   I. Title.
RG560.W35 2007   2006037160
618.2'00[B]92—dc22

Printed in the United States of America
1 3 5 7 9 10 8 6 4 2

BOOK DESIGN BY AMANDA DEWEY

While the author has made every effort to provide accurate telephone numbers and
Internet addresses at the time of publication, neither the publisher nor the author
assumes any responsibility for errors, or for changes that occur after publication. Further, the publisher does not have any control over and does not assume any responsibility for author or third-party websites or their content.

For Tenzin,
who made it real

Myths are public dreams, dreams are private myths. . . .

Joseph Campbell

BABYLOVE

April 8

I'm pregnant.

I just got off the phone with the nurse from Dr. Lowen's office. I picked up the old brown Trimline phone that's been in this retreat cabin of my mother's forever, and a woman's voice asked for me and I said, This is she, and the voice said, It's Becky from Dr. Lowen's office. And I said, Uh-huh. Then Becky said, The result from the latest test was positive, and I said, Positive? And she said, Yes, you are no longer borderline pregnant.

No longer borderline pregnant? I thought I might fall over. I looked out the window at the leaves of the poplar trees shimmering in the breeze. My eyes settled on a vulture falling from the sky in a perfect spiral. He was flapping then gliding, flapping then gliding as he descended, and I thought to myself: I will remember this moment and that vulture for the rest of my life. I thought to myself: That vulture is a sign. A part of me is dying.

And then the nurse said, Hello? And I said, Yes, I am here. Are you sure I am pregnant? And she said, Yes. And I said, Really? Are you sure? You're not going call me back in two hours and say you made a mistake? She said, No. And I said, Well, how do you know? She sighed. It was a ridiculous question, but since she had been telling me for a week that after three blood draws they still couldn't tell if I was really pregnant, I felt justified. So I pushed. Well, what do you know today that you didn't yesterday? And she said, The HCG levels are definitely going up. HCG levels? Yes, in the last twenty-four hours the pregnancy hormone count has risen from 700 to over 2,300, and that usually means a healthy, robust beginning.

And then I had what could only be the first twinges of the maternal instinct. Healthy and robust? A huge smile spread across my face. That's my baby! And then it was as if the synapses in my brain sending exploratory signals to my uterus finally made contact. Aye, mate, is it a go down there? Yes, yes, Captain, we're full steam ahead!

I was convinced that getting off the phone would exponentially increase my chances of reverting to not-pregnant, but I released Becky anyway and stumbled over to the bathroom, where Glen, my life partner and father of our soon-to-be-born baby, was shaving. I looked into his eyes and tried to keep myself from screaming and jumping up and down. We did it, I said. He grinned. Well, I guess that puts the whole motility question to rest. And I said, I guess it does. Then I wrapped my arms around him and buried my face in his chest, and he wrapped his arms around me and rested his chin on the top of my head.

I was in ecstatic bliss for about ninety seconds, and then it hit me: an avalanche of dread that took my breath away. Pregnant? A baby? What have I done? I looked at Glen. He was going through his own reality check, which brought me even closer to the brink of total hysteria. But then, before I could burst into tears and run screaming out of the room, he pulled me into his arms. You are going to be a fantastic mother, he said to me, to my fear. His love overwhelmed me, and I started to cry big, wet tears onto his favorite black shirt.

We're going to have a baby.

One

FOR THE LAST FIFTEEN YEARS I have told everyone—friends, family, hairdressers, editors, cabdrivers, doctors, and anyone else who would listen—that I wanted a baby. *I want to have a baby,* I would say with urgency or a wistful longing, or both. And I meant what I said, I really did, I just had no idea what I was talking about. I had almost no actual experience of babies, so the object of my wanting was abstract, the display of it ritualized. *I want to have a baby* was something I said, a statement that evoked a trajectory, a general direction for my life.

The truth is, I was wracked with ambivalence. I had the usual questions: When, with whom, and how the hell was I going to afford it? But there was something else, too, a question common—if not always conscious—to women of my generation, women raised to view motherhood with more than a little suspicion. Can I survive having a baby? Will I lose myself—my body, my mind, my *options*—and be left trapped, resentful, and irretrievably overwhelmed? If I have a baby, we wonder silently to ourselves, will I die?

To compound matters, I had a tempestuous relationship with my mother, and feared the inevitable kickback sure to follow such a final and dramatic departure from daughterhood. What if, instead of joy and excitement, my mother felt threatened by the baby, and pushed even further into the margins of my life? What if, then, out of jealousy and her own discontent, she launched covert or not-so-covert strikes against my irrefutable separateness, now symbolized so completely by becoming a mother myself?

Because mothers make us, because they map our emotional terrain before we even know we are capable of having an emotional terrain, they know just where to stick the dynamite. With a few small power plays—a skeptical comment, the withholding of approval or praise—a mother can devastate a daughter. Decades of subtle undermining can stunt a daughter, or so monopolize her energy that she in effect stunts herself. Muted, fearful, riddled with self-doubt, she can remain trapped in daughterhood forever, the one place she feels confident she knows the rules.

I was not the only daughter in a dyad of this kind. When I looked around, I saw them everywhere: in my extended family, at my lectures on college campuses, on line at Target, on their own show on TV. Childless and codependent, the daughter did some macabre human version of dying on the vine. The mother kept the reality of her own mortality at bay by thwarting her daughter's every attempt to psychologically leave the nest.

It seemed that these mothers did not realize that they had to *give* adulthood to their daughters by stepping down, stepping back, stepping away, and letting the daughter take center stage. These mothers did not seem to know, with all their potions and philosophies, their desires to rehabilitate ancient scripts of gender and identity, that there is a natural order, and that natural order involves passing the scepter to offspring with unconditional love and pride.

Or pay the price.

BECAUSE AS A WRITER I do my best research on the lives of others, at least once a week I sat conversing—over tea, on subway platforms, at the farmers' market, in ornate, fancy hotel lobbies—about motherhood with women who either had done the deed and lived to tell, or who were surveying the same terrain of possibility.

I spoke to single moms and partnered moms, and moms who lost their children to disease. I spoke to stay-at-home moms, working moms, CEO moms, moms on welfare. One mom I met conceived through in vitro fertilization at age forty-five. Another orchestrated different sperm donors over several pregnancies. One "got pregnant" at eighteen and spent the rest of her life trying to recover. I spent an afternoon talking with a poor mom who relied on faith to provide for her sixth child on the way. I spent several years talking to middle-class moms who couldn't figure out how to support the two kids they had been raising for years.

I talked to men, too, about the joys and risks of parenthood, but my time with them was different. It wasn't punctuated with anecdotes, or even held together by narrative. Men explored the topic of my pregnancy with meaningful glances and gentle touches of assurance to the small of my back. They encouraged me with knowing nods and unwavering attention, sometimes silently offering themselves, other times letting me know they wished it could be them.

Women gave me narrative and men gave me alchemy, their approbation running like a current into my womb.

My life was full of these elucidating encounters, but strangely, none of them seemed to bring me any closer to what I said I wanted. Unconsciously, I longed to give birth to a child. Consciously, I managed the risk of actually having one by viewing it as one option among many, a wonderful possibility to peruse at will. Like choosing which coast to live on or what apartment to take, I would consider potential outcomes and make my best, informed decision.

Because I am a woman of privilege, a product of the women's movement, and a student of cultural relativism, I believed that neither choice would be inherently better than the other. Each had pluses and minuses, and so it would not be the choice itself, but how I interpreted the choice that would make the difference. Los Angeles or New York? High floor or great location? To baby or not to baby?

Ultimately, it was like trying to steer a boat with a banana. I had no idea what was going on, no clue whatsoever. I didn't know that I was already in the water, that the tide was coming in fast, and that I had no option other than to be taken out to sea. I didn't know that the longing, fear, and ambivalence were part of the pregnancy, the birth, and everything that came after. I didn't know that the showdown between the ideas of my mother's generation and my own was inescapable, and slated to play out personally in our relationship. I didn't know that those fifteen years constituted my real first trimester, and all that time my baby was coming toward me, and I was moving toward my baby.

What I did know is that I had mothered or tried to mother every single human being who had crossed my path—including the son of my former partner of six years—to the point of absurdity, exhaustion, and everything in between. What I did know is that one year in a stunning turquoise lagoon in Mexico, I had a vision of two babies, my babies, and at the very moment their copper faces smiled at me in my mind's eye, two tiny silver fish leapt out of the ocean, inches from my lips. What I did know is that even though I doubted my ability to mother, partner, work, evolve, and serve, all in one lifetime, some part of this flesh body I call me was being pulled toward birth: my baby's and my own.

You may not look pregnant at this point but your embryo's heart, no bigger than a poppyseed, has already begun to beat and pump blood. . . . The embryo itself is about a quarter of an inch long and looks more like a tadpole than a human.

April 10

I called my mother last night to tell her the news, because I promised she would be the first to know. When I told her I have never been happier, she was quiet. She said she was shocked, which was shocking to me since I've been telling her for a year that all I want is to write books and have babies. When we were about to hang up, she asked me to check her garden. I said okay and told her that I had ordered some outdoor lights for this tiny house she lets me use, and that the new tile in the shower is almost finished. Then I hung up and started to cry.

I don't know if I wanted her to be like all the other mothers I've seen get the news, whooping for joy and crying and jumping up and down, but when she didn't, I was overcome with doubt. Flopping down on the bed, I regressed all the way back to high school, when I got my acceptance letter from Yale. I was ecstatic, and proudly presented the letter to my mother as she cooked dinner. She calmly husked a few ears of corn, and then asked why I would want to go to a conservative bastion of male privilege. It didn't take ten seconds for me to question my own dreams. Why *did* I want to go to one of the most well-respected colleges in the world?

Why *am* I having a baby?

Glen found me lying on the floor, practically catatonic, staring out into space with tears streaming down my face. We talked for a long time about rites of passage, and how everyone is bound to have a reaction that has nothing to do with me. Mothers and fathers have to reckon with their own mortality, with becoming grandparents, and what that means about where they are in the life cycle. He told me to get ready, people say the strangest things when you tell them you are pregnant because it brings up so much for them.

Like when I met with my literary agent about this book. She told me she was pregnant with her third baby, and I said something awful like, How can you possibly take care of three children? Or even worse, Was it an accident? Then I grilled her on whether she would be able to take care of her baby, my book, and me. I was seized with anxiety in the moment, but really, her pregnancy rang my bell. Happy, vibrant, strong, direct. I thought, If she can be a VP of her company, gaze adoringly at a photo of her husband whipped out of her purse, and talk about how her kids are the greatest gifts of her life, this baby thing must be possible.

I went to sleep pondering whether I got more positive messaging about having a baby from my agent in thirty-five minutes than I did from my mother in thirty-five years.

April 13

I'm back in Berkeley, in my apartment that suddenly looks like a broom closet. Where am I going to put a crib?

Dr. Lowen ordered an ultrasound this morning to make sure that there really is a baby growing inside me. Isn't that why I'd asked Becky ten times if she was sure? Dr. Lowen says we need to know that the fetus is inside my uterus and not ectopic. *Ectopic!* Glen had to calm me down. All I could think was that a problem must have showed up on the last blood test and Dr. Lowen didn't want to tell me on the phone and give me heart failure.

Glen drove me to the hospital, and then tried to distract me in the waiting room with bad jokes and blueberries. I kept asking him what we'd do if the baby were ectopic, if I lost the baby before I even had her. How is it possible to feel so attached so soon? By the time the technician called my name, I was sure it was all going to end in tragedy. She poked and rubbed and scanned and prodded my uterus for about twenty minutes, looking for the tiny cluster of cells and shaking her head until I was convinced the whole thing was a fluke. At that exact moment, when I squeezed Glen's hand and said, Well, maybe we don't have a baby after all, the technician pushed the button on her mouse ball and drew a line from one point to the other. Got it.

So now it's super-duper official. I've got a baby growing in my uterus. It's really the most surreal, ridiculous, amazing thing.

April 15

Rushed around, getting ready to fly to Minneapolis to speak on the importance of mentorship in young women's lives at the Minnesota

Conference on Adolescent Females. Usually I like going to Minneapolis, but today I am just so tired. I can't imagine getting on a plane and then turning around the next day to come back. It's only three and a half hours each way, but at the moment, Minnesota may as well be the North Pole.

I was up all night consumed with anxiety about money—mine and every other mother's. By most standards I am well off, but now that all I do is think about the stuff I am going to have to pay for, like the college education that's going to cost two million dollars in eighteen years, I don't know. I remember my mother making endless calculations on brown paper bags and blank pages in her journal when I was a child, and my father sitting at the dining-room table writing checks out every month, his brow furrowed and intense. They must have felt the same way, going over the numbers again and again, wondering how it was all going to work out.

I woke up feeling guilty for even thinking about all this. Most people in the world raise their children with far less than I have. But that's the thing, isn't it? Even when you have enough money to pay for nonessentials like organic produce and designer toothpaste, there is still the yawning fear of not having, losing everything, living in deprivation.

I definitely thought about money long before this baby moved into my womb. I worried about how we were going to send my ex-girlfriend's son, Solomon, to boarding school. I worried about how much health insurance costs, and how little money I put into my IRA. But now my thinking has a frightening urgency. I find myself wondering how all the other pregnant women and mothers and fathers manage what basically boils down to sheer terror in the face of so much responsibility. Religion suddenly makes a lot more sense. So does workaholism. And Xanax. And back-to-the-land movements that emphasize doing more with less.

I bolted out of bed this morning to research the Voluntary Simplicity movement. I read dozens of entries by people named Sinnan and Marigold who grow their own food, wear only three pairs of pants, and make their own soap. I learned that an American baby consumes two hundred times more of the earth's resources than a baby from Eritrea.

By the time Glen woke up, I was deep in my closet, figuring out how many pairs of shoes and sweaters I could transform into fossil fuel in order to justify having an American baby. When he asked what I was doing, I snapped that I was freaking out about money, wasn't that obvious? He sat in the big chair in our bedroom and put his feet up, watching me. I mean really, I said, how are we going to put this baby through college?

He paused. There are always student loans. Student loans? I said, lifting my head out of a storage bin at the back of the closet. I had forgotten about those. Weren't several of my friends still paying off their student loans, and didn't they seem as neurotic and happy as anybody else? I gently extracted a purple sweater from the giveaway pile.

Having a partner who thinks rationally and optimistically even when I cannot does not eliminate my anxiety about supporting another human being for the next twenty years, but it certainly helps.

April 22

I made it back from Minneapolis last night in one piece, but this morning I almost killed myself with a spritz of perfume. I've been trying to ignore the growing intensity of my reaction to smells, but today I just couldn't. I took off all my clothes, got back in the shower, and scrubbed off the barest hint of perfume I had put on my neck. Then I drove to my homeopath's office grumbling about what a bummer it is that I can't wear scent without feeling like I am on a capsizing catamaran.

Marie's excitement cheered me up. I feel it's her victory, too, because from the moment I said I wanted to have a baby, she's been right there with me, giving me flower tinctures and vitamin D, progesterone tablets and visualizations of myself big and pregnant with a happy, healthy baby.

After the hugs and whoops, I confessed that I almost gave up on our noninvasive plan because I thought that after six months, I wasn't getting any younger and should try the medical model. I told her that I had already scheduled the HSG (hysterosalpingogram), where they inject dye into your fallopian tubes to see if they work, and I had a prescription for the ovulation-inducing Clomid in my bag. It was the preliminary, precautionary pregnancy test Dr. Lowen ordered that revealed the fruit of our homeopathic work.

Marie didn't bat an eye or get judgmental, and that's why I love her, my kindhearted M.D. homeopath. She just said, Well, good thing you didn't have to go through all of that! and started making a list of all the foods I should start eating: farm-raised lamb, eggs, Norwegian fish oil.

Then we talked about whether I should stop taking the low-dose antidepressant I've been taking to counteract God-knows-how-many generations of depression in my family tree. The thought of quitting cold turkey is terrifying. I have gone from being skeptical of my little purple pill, to angry that I need it, to hugely grateful to all of the good people in big pharma involved in creating it. I'm not exaggerating when I say it has allowed me to have some semblance of a normal life.

As I looked on expectantly, Marie checked her big pharmaceutical handbook to see if trials have been done on pregnant women. Limited trials, she said, but the drug is rated B for pregnancy, which means it's not stellar, but it is doable. I looked at her across the desk covered with mugs, supplements, and files. Unless we know for sure that it will hurt the baby, I said, I just don't think it's a good idea for me to stop. The first thing depression takes from me is hope, and I am pretty sure I can't have a baby without that. She agreed.

I left her office feeling good about the decision, but still full of concern. In addition to all of the other ways I can lose or harm this baby, I can now add the possibility of damaging his nervous system with what to some is an optional drug.

I also wonder about straddling the medical ob/gyn and homeopathic worlds. In theory they are compatible, but in reality I am not so sure. Dr. Lowen is all business and efficiency, Formica and fluorescents, and Marie is soft lighting and colorful art, hugs and flower remedies. Of course, Marie says they are compatible—after all, she is an M.D.—and Dr. Lowen tries to sound sympathetic when I mention the natural methods. But in real life, there seems to be an eerie disconnect between the two that leaves me slightly uncertain about both.

Which brings me back to where I started, at the perfume that triggered today's initial bout of uncertainty about what just might be the biggest decision I've ever made. Is this the beginning of the end? Is this the first of many things I love that I will have to give up for the baby? First perfume and then sanity, sleep, and travel to interesting places? Is this what everybody means when they say your life will never be the same? Say goodbye to emotional stability? Say goodbye to amber, lavender, rose, and sandalwood? Say goodbye to Brooklyn, Paris, and Dakar?

Is there any peace in this process? I struggled for years to decide whether to even become a parent. Now that it's happening, I'm plagued by apocalyptic visions of how it's going to turn out. Has it always been this way? Is this elixir of ambivalence and anxiety the universal experience of motherhood, or is it just America, circa right now?

Two

MANY WOMEN SAY that for as long as they can remember, they've wanted to have a baby. They say that playing with dolls was their first introduction to the idea of motherhood, that they've known since childhood they would give birth.

I didn't play with dolls. I never knew, the way I knew that I would go to college and eventually earn a living, that I would have a baby. Unlike those women who can't pinpoint exactly how or why they came to the feeling, I remember exactly when and where I felt the first pang of maternal desire.

I was in Africa, on a continent so foreign that none of my old thoughts about myself could hold. I found I could live without running water and electricity. I could survive armed soldiers and random searches of my bags on public buses. I could be friends, sisters even, with women who covered themselves from head to toe in swaths of black cloth.

And, because of a man I met, I could fantasize about having a child.

Ade was and still is a devout Muslim. We met in the middle of Ramadan and spent hours on the rooftop of my guesthouse talking about his culture. In conversations I dominated, I questioned him pointedly about how women were treated. What were his thoughts about the veil? Forget niceties. I wanted to know: Were the women in his family circumcised? I asked these questions, but I can't say I was open to Ade's answers. Though only twenty years old, I was positive I knew much more than Ade about the gender politics of his country from the books I had read and women I had befriended.

But Ade wasn't affected by my arrogance. He listened to each of my criticisms intently, and responded with a rather (compared to mine) complex view. He told me first what he believed (women are as powerful as men and should be respected as equals), and then explained what the Quran taught (one of the Prophet's wives was a businesswoman who financed his rise), and then finally conceded the interpretation of those with power (women should be subordinate and obedient). He was adamant that there was no circumcision, but promised to ask Fatima, a rare female friend with whom he could talk about these things, and tell me what she said.

What can I say? I fell for Ade during those conversations. Ade could talk. He wasn't afraid of me. He seemed to know his own mind, to have considered the issues I raised and come to some decisions, decisions I respected even if I didn't agree. He was unfamiliar with the intellectual combat I was honing at college, and his lack of competitiveness allowed me a relaxed curiosity I had not known. When he left, I felt awake and alive, as if the door of everything I had learned had been blown open.

Because of this and other factors too numerous to mention here, I stayed several months with Ade, and one day, after I had convinced my traveling companion to go to Tanzania without me and I no longer knew when I would leave Ade's tiny island or why, I went out in a dhow with Ade and some friends. We were far from the shore, out on the open sea. I was wearing a gray T-shirt and Ade's blue-and-white-striped *kikoi* around my waist. Ade was balancing himself on the hull of the boat, releasing the rope that let the ship's battered sail unfurl in the wind.

As the boat picked up speed, I leaned back on my elbows and imagined a future with Ade. Even though his culture and beliefs ran up against everything I knew and held sacred, I found myself fantasizing that I would spend the rest of my life with him, that I would wash clothes by hand in a basin with two cups of water, and give up reading at night because we wouldn't have electricity. I dreamed that I would dress modestly and respect his mother, that I would learn to cook delicious food in huge aluminum pots over an open fire.

And then the fantasy I'd never had: the dream that was less about Ade than it was about what I suddenly saw as possible for my life. I would have a baby with Ade, two babies, three babies, as many babies as I could.

A baby. I want to have a baby.

And then, just as quickly, I turned my eyes from the sky to the floor of the old boat and thought, *That's ridiculous. I can't have a baby. I have to finish school and start my career.*

April 25

I'm back in Mendocino. The drive up from Berkeley last night was *awful*. I was so nauseated going around the curves, we had to stop the car. As I leaned out the window gulping air and smelling the blood of fresh roadkill thirty feet away, I thought seriously about walking, or going to sleep in the backseat and trying again in the morning. I was so happy to get to the gate to the house. I threw myself on the ground and lay there smelling the dirt and waiting for the world to stop spinning.

I'm nauseated and exhausted, but none of that has any effect whatsoever on my urge to nest. I know I'm always trying to make a home because I moved so many times as a kid, but now my nesting thing is on, like, hyperturbo overdrive. My mind just goes tick, tick, tick across every room, scanning for possible upgrades and nooks that could be softer, more comfortable, more homey.

After we unpacked the bags and bags of food, and after I set up my desk by hooking up my laptop and getting the lamp positioned just so, I checked the shower tile and the light fixtures. Then I went around and made a list of the other changes I needed to talk to Carl, my friend the builder/contractor, about.

I don't know how he does it, but Glen just reads and eats and relaxes as I run around trying to make everything perfect. By just leaving me alone, he gives me permission to be myself and I *love* that. I feel the animal aspect of it, too. I am making the nest and he's standing over, protecting all three of us while I do it.

April 28

Today I feel sad, tired, and unsure about everything. Like I have no real support outside of Glen for having this baby. Like I have no healthy models for how to have a family. My parents barely spoke to each other for twenty-five years. After raising two children together, my father and stepmother live somewhat separate lives. My relationships thus far have been, um, educational, but not terribly successful.

I am trying not to ruminate on all of this and to believe that I can reverse the divorce dynamic by staying with Glen until one of us dies, but it's like my mind is in a vise. When I am not throwing up or wanting to throw up, I am having anxiety attacks about being homeless, unable to keep my family together, and making the same mistakes my parents made. Other variations on the doomsday theme running through my mind: miscarriage, miscarriage, and miscarriage.

I would rather die than hurt my baby, but I think I would actually die if I lost my baby.

Is that a depressed thought or a normal pregnancy feeling?

April 30

Today I was outrageously nauseated, but went looking at gates with Carl anyway. I think I can safely describe Carl as an aging hippie. He built many houses in Anderson Valley and along the Mendocino coast, and is incredibly knowledgeable about all things having to do with construction, environmental preservation, and a host of other things we haven't yet talked about. He's in his sixties, and has a little shake that makes hitting nails a challenge sometimes, but I consider it a blessing that he has agreed to help reclaim this little house of my mother's from dry rot, wasps, and a general state of dilapidation.

After finding a fairly nice gate that I will be able to open and shut without too much effort even at nine months, we went to see the house he has been building for his family for fifteen years. His wife, Martine, made me chamomile tea with honey for the nausea I told her was flattening me, and Carl brought over a book of photographs of the home birth of his second child.

The pictures were incredible. Carl was young and cute, with long, braided hippie hair and an embroidered denim shirt. In the pictures, he's rubbing his wife's back and holding her hand and kissing her. She's lying down, fully naked and fully pregnant, surrendering to the process first on her back, then on her side, then on all fours when the baby is ready to come out. The room is dim so the baby won't be shocked, and Carl's first child, Tomas, who was four or five, holds a flashlight so they can take pictures.

Martine and Carl sent me home with something called *The Birth Book,* a collection of birth stories published by a midwifery collective Carl worked with in the seventies. After reading the stories of ten or fifteen women and their partners and midwives, I feel more than ever that I want to have a home birth. I can't imagine having the baby in a hospital. I just don't see how lying flat on your back can possibly be the best way to have a baby. I mean, for starters, it works *against* gravity.

May 4

I had my first official prenatal appointment today. It was like being on a conveyor belt at the baby-making factory. I was weighed, my urine tested, and seven vials of blood were extracted from my arm. I was asked about my mother's health, my father's, sister's, and brother's. Then back to the beginning for Glen's family info. The doctor briefly skipped a rock across the ocean of my diet, instructing me to avoid shellfish, raw eggs, and one other thing that I now cannot remember. Then she prescribed a prenatal vitamin and handed me several sample packets of the enormous bright purple pill. She did a quick vaginal exam, apparently the only one I am going to have until I go into labor, and then the whole thing was over.

The appointment took about twenty-five minutes and she never looked at or touched my stomach. There wasn't time or opportunity to discuss the creeping depression I've been feeling, or how concerned I am about my life changing, or my fear that I won't be able to handle it all. I mean, technically there was. She did ask how I was feeling, but we were going along at such a clip, I couldn't imagine what would happen if I bogged things down with my actual thoughts. She did say she had several patients who stayed on antidepressants through their pregnancies with no side effects whatsoever. That was helpful, considering I've been gnashing my teeth to stubs every night worrying about the implications of taking them: Am I going to burn in hell or give my kid epilepsy?

She also said, somewhere in between the questions about my family's health history and the exam, that she's looking forward to delivering my baby. And that she hopes I won't do something silly, like have a home birth.

Uh-huh.

After the prenatal, I indulged in my bimonthly luxury of getting my eyebrows and toes done. Just as I was lying down, Yelena, who has been in charge of my eyebrows for the last three years, asked how old I am and if I am planning to have children. I hesitated just a second too long, trying to figure out how to answer, and she said, You're pregnant! And I said, Yes, and she said, I knew it! And then we both laughed and I told her how nauseated and tired and freaked out I am, and she told me about her clients who come in to the salon the day before their due date to get a Brazilian bikini wax. Apparently, they want to look good for the doctors. By the time I left, my toes were a lovely lilac and I was laughing my head off.

May 6

The mood swings are so intense. I woke up at four in the morning and scribbled this on the back of a paper bag:

> I am eight weeks pregnant and terrified. Each morning
> I wake up filled with a peculiar blend of dread and longing.
> Who am I, and what the hell is happening to me? Already
> I eat uncontrollably, craving foods I classified as off-limits
> years ago: huge balls of mozzarella, thick steaks dripping
> with blood, slice after slice of eggplant. After only eight

weeks, my breasts are painful to the touch, my small nipples now engorged to twice their normal size and dark as blackberries. I cannot drive to the store without having to slow the car to twenty in a fifty-mile-per-hour zone, without pulling over at a gas station to let the ocean of nausea subside. To make matters worse, I can no longer get into my favorite pair of jeans, and my hard-won good posture, the result of hundreds of Alexander Technique lessons, seems frightfully on the sway. And oh yeah, forget about planes, which I have to board every other week to give lectures, readings, and writing workshops. Just the words "jet" and "fuel" send me running for the toilet.

And that's just my body. Far worse is what my mind is doing to me. In my worst moments, when I am seeing my patient and adoring partner as a modern-day Satan, and feeling as if I am going to be an unfit joke of a mother, I am certain that I am being invaded by alien intelligence, a force so powerful it can make me do things I otherwise would not, a force so totally in control of me, I may never know who I am again. And while daddy-to-be can make eggs and burn the turkey bacon just like I like it, he can't really help with the psychological plunges I keep having to claw my way out of because after all, I am going to be this child's mother, and heaven help me and her if I can't figure out how to contain my anxiety about it. Right?

Of course, being the writer and reader and info-junkie that we all are these days, I've bought a half-dozen books to try to get myself through this. I've scoured all 669,801 pages on the Internet on pregnancy and the first trimester, pregnancy and depression, pregnancy and emotions, pregnancy and anxiety, pregnancy and fear. They all, every one of them, allow for the kinds of mood swings I am having, they all say that everything I am feeling and thinking is normal, healthy, and won't hurt the baby. But while the experts say what I want to hear, they still don't seem to say it as adamantly as I need them to. They don't say, Yes, you may feel as if you are going to lose your mind and there will be moments when you reconsider everything and think, after all this wanting and trying and hoping and thinking about names and strollers and birthing methods, that the only reasonable thing to do at this point is terminate the pregnancy.

They don't tell you that. Or if they do, they tell you in tones so soft and modest and reserved and professional that you want to scream at the page, the computer, the doctor, Yes, but do you understand that this whole thing is *freaking me out*? My life is about to change and *I have no idea how to prepare*? And do you know why they are calm and you are not? Because they don't have to have this baby, you do. They are not going to be responsible for this being for the rest of their lives, you are. They are not going to lie in bed worrying about the week of doxycycline you took before you knew you were pregnant and whether or not the baby is going to have stained teeth that need forty thousand dollars' worth of veneers. They are going to go home at the end of the day without carrying your baby with them. You will never be able to go home at the end of the day without carrying your baby again.

Cheery, huh?

May 7

Went to see the Tibetan doctor I have been trying to get an appointment with for months. She's in town for only four or five days every two weeks. Her office was in a cramped suite at the top of a dark stair in a nondescript building on an exceedingly plain street. I chatted a little with a woman in a wheelchair in the waiting room, who told me she has been seeing the doctor for years and swears by her. Everyone else I talk to about her says the same thing. That she comes from a long line of doctors—her father is one of the Dalai Lama's private physicians—and she's incredible.

After forty-five minutes, she appeared and invited me into the inner office. I sat at the foot of the examination table in a wooden chair and told her I was pregnant and super-nauseated and super-tired and maybe just a tiny bit more anxious than usual. She nodded and took my pulse. Then I said, Well, maybe I am way more anxious than usual, and a bit depressed, and she nodded again and asked me to stick out my tongue. She asked me a few more questions about my diet and what times of the day I feel best and worst.

Then she said that there is still a chance I can lose the baby, and that I should keep my stomach and the rest of my body warm. She gave me a list of warming foods to eat, and herbal pellets to quiet the nausea, ease the anxiety, and clear my system of damp, cold, and clogging elements. She told me to make a drink of pomegranate juice, ginger tea, and honey, and to take 300 mg of liquid magnesium a day. She said I should consider going off the antidepressant.

Uh, really?

When I came out carrying my little silk bags of herbs and a sheaf of instructions, Glen was waiting for me. He was skeptical about the herbs. He wanted to make sure they wouldn't hurt the baby. I got upset and told him that this doctor has been treating people for years and years and that I didn't think she would give me something that would damage the baby. I told him what she said about the antidepressant, and he said I should choose one doctor and follow him or her. He said that all of this doctor-hopping was really just a manifestation of my fear of my life changing and how overwhelming and uncontrollable it all is. He said that if I am not careful, I could end up hurting myself or the baby, or both.

I burst into tears.

He may be right, but it's weird to have to listen to someone else's concerns about what I do with my body. Even though I get theoretically that it's Glen's baby, too, at the moment it's still a bit abstract. Yesterday he reminded me, after I called the baby mine one too many times, that I *am* appearing on national TV and radio promoting my latest book on masculinity and saying that men need to be more involved with every aspect of domestic life and women need to let them.

Which made me wonder, am I being a hypocrite when I think, Just let me deal with the baby in my body, you go get food and protect me while I'm doing it? It feels sacrilegious to think it, blasphemous to write it down, but maybe there is something to this whole biology thing.

Needless to say, I had a splitting headache by the time I got home. I took three of my new pellets, one of each kind. I had to crack one of them open with my teeth and chew it up. It tasted like dirt mixed with, I don't know, cyanide?

I HAVE BEEN sleeping for eight hours and now I am *starving*. I find the incessant desire to eat, no matter how shitty I am feeling, both fascinating and annoying. It's as if the baby doesn't care what I am going through, she's going to make it here no matter what.

May 8

On what I can already tell is going to be the first of many outings in search of pregnancy clothes that don't make me look like an infantilized suburban housewife, today I went to a shop called Japanese Weekend. It was recommended by one of my more stylish friends, and so it was in anticipation of the Prada of maternity wear that I made my way up Powell Street. What I found was a modest shop with six or seven racks of black, white, denim, and khaki pants and one Asian-styled top in several cheery prints.

At first I was disappointed. I just couldn't get excited about the same plain pants in four colors, all with a thick elastic band around the waist. But then Blanca, the very gentle and attentive saleswoman, suggested I try the pants in a small changing room and nodded approvingly at my reflection when I did. As she admired, I berated myself for being such a snob. The pants were fantastic, and I decided in a matter of seconds that I was never taking them off.

In my determination to "network with other moms to ensure the success of my baby," as advised by the editors of the *Fit Pregnancy* magazine I scoured in my ob/gyn's waiting room, I started talking to the other trying-to-stay-cool mamas trying on pants. One woman was five months "along" and had a gigantic one-year-old knocked out in a stroller. Even though she couldn't stop herself from telling me that her son was in the ninety-fifth percentile for weight and height for his age group, I was terribly impressed with this mom. She was dressed casually, in a simple black T-shirt and jeans, and had her dark, curly hair pulled back in a ponytail. She was confident and friendly and seemed very down to earth. She had great cheekbones and lovely lips that were lightly rouged.

Because she wasn't the total mess I expect a woman with a baby in a stroller and one on the way to be, I asked for her secret. She said humor and a stay-at-home husband. Then she began extolling the virtues of the Japanese Weekend pant, namely the elastic band that sits below the belly and can be folded over in the later months. I fell more in love with her when she called the pants she was looking for a "piece," and then pulled the pants she thought would be good for me from the sale rack.

The second mom-to-be to share the mirror was a little more high-strung. She looked like a corporate lawyer on her lunch break, and she tore through the options Blanca handed her with alacrity. We asked each other what I have surmised to be the stock mom-to-be questions: How many months, is this your first, do you know if it's a girl or a boy, and have you picked a name? She was four months pregnant with her first, a girl, with no name. When I congratulated her and said, "Oh how exciting, you're having a girl!" she grimaced and said, "Well, I don't know, girls are easier in the beginning but much harder later on. You know, the whole mother-daughter thing." I was so shocked by her candor that I just nodded and ducked back into the dressing cubicle. But I can't stop thinking about what she said. I just want my baby to be healthy, but I know what she means.

May 9

Mother's Day.

Went with my mother to see a documentary about a guy who eats McDonald's food for thirty days. After the film, I told her that

I've been feeling depressed, and she told me she was depressed throughout her pregnancy. She said that she always assumed it was because she was isolated in Mississippi, where I was born and where she was working with my father in the civil rights movement, but maybe it was hormonal and genetically so. She said she was practically suicidal, and there were days and days she couldn't get out of bed. She said between the nausea (check) and the depression (double check), she almost lost her mind.

When I spoke with my father on the phone last night, he confirmed her memory. I asked how he dealt with it, and he said, Well, it was hard. Then he told me a story I'd never heard:

My mother wanted to go to Mexico after her first trimester because she was convinced that the sun and getting out of Mississippi would make her feel better. The only problem was that they didn't have any money. So my father put their car, the VW Bug his mother bought him when he graduated from law school, up for sale. *Your car?* I screech. You sold *your car* to go on a trip to Mexico? He laughs, not quite able to believe it, either. We lived in a suburb. My father's office was blocks and blocks away, as was the grocery store and just about everything else. He said it seemed so important to my mother, and he knew he could get a loaner from work. So they sold the Bug and went to Mexico, where they bought two paintings by the now famous Mexican painter Rufino Tamayo and got nauseated riding on public buses careening around mountain curves.

I asked my father if my mother's depression lifted as a result of the trip. I think I remember a picture of her in Mexico, wearing a red-and-white serape and a huge smile. He is silent for a long moment. You know, Rebec, I can't remember. I don't think so.

Shit.

May 12

I broke the bank today at the market. I bought three different kinds of prenatal vitamins, two bottles of nausea-quelling ginger syrup, a box of healthy-pregnancy tea, two whole cooked chickens, two dozen eggs, bunches and bunches of kale, spinach, and broccoli, a huge piece of halibut, two containers of tuna, two Caesar salads, two containers each of blueberries and strawberries, tomatoes, carrots, and about six different kinds of organic chocolate, including a pound of fruit-sweetened chocolate-covered raisins. I have no doubt that if I had more arms, time, and money, I would have filled five more carts. I can't tell if I was hungry, slightly manic, or revved up with pregnancy hormones.

I rushed home to meet Sonam, my potential midwife, whom I have known for years and always imagined delivering my baby. She arrived with her granddaughter asleep in a stroller just as I was unpacking the last grocery bag, took her shoes off, and asked if she could brush her teeth. Then we sat around my kitchen table with a calendar trying to figure out how pregnant I am. I told her Dr. Lowen's estimate of eight weeks from the ultrasound, and that I think I am more like ten weeks. She took notes about how I have been feeling (tired, nauseated, depressed) while I made tea and devoured a container of tuna and a whole box of crackers.

When her granddaughter woke up, we shifted into the bedroom and talked some more while the baby went around the bedroom picking up my shoes and letting them fall to the floor with a boom that made her laugh. It was great to have a real live baby in the house, a prelude to what is to come. Since Sonam is a friend of both my mother and me, and because she asked, I told her that my mom wasn't as enthusiastic as I had hoped. She told me to remember that whatever is going on with my mother has nothing to do with me, and that babies have a way of transforming families. She also said depression is common, especially in the first trimester, and that I should boost my vitamin B intake to help.

Then, get this, I lay down on *my very own* bed, and she felt my stomach, measuring the size of my uterus by counting thumb-widths from my belly button. The second she put her hands on my belly, I knew that I wanted her to deliver the baby. It was like she was talking to the baby with her hands, and the baby was listening. And I felt so safe, like I could fall apart and scream and cry and freak out with her, and she would know what to do.

Lying there, I thought more about how much I want to have this baby at home. The one video of a birth I have seen is of a woman giving birth to her baby in a hot tub with just her husband attending. She goes into labor and she's totally calm, doing deep breathing and walking around their house looking like she's in another dimension. As the contractions get more intense, she hangs on her husband's shoulders and he massages her back. Then she gets into the hot tub and out comes the baby, looking unbothered and serene.

My mother said she wished that my birth could have been like that, instead of in the newly desegregated hospital with the doctor she didn't like, who gave her an episiotomy she may not have needed. My mother's experience haunts me. I am terrified of being cut. Episiotomy, C-section, I just don't want to be lying there helpless and at the mercy of a bunch of doctors in a hurry to get to their golf game.

May 14

I flew to Seattle yesterday to keynote the annual benefit dinner for the Northwest Women's Law Center. I talked about how since I've been pregnant, I've been more concerned than ever about the need for people in politics and the public eye to have healthy personal lives. So often the momentous cultural work happens at the expense of family and sustained intimacy with loved ones. I saw a lot of heads nodding as I spoke, and several couples came up afterward to talk about their experiences trying to keep their families together in the midst of giving so much of themselves to the work they care so much about.

I met some interesting people at the dinner, including a judge who told me about the evisceration of the Equal Employment Opportunity Commission, and the loveliest woman who was seven months pregnant. Of course we had a pregnancy moment because I can't stop myself from telling every single person I meet my news, and pregnant women? Forget it. It's all I can do not to grab them and sit them down in a corner somewhere to pump them for info about the road ahead. The vast, miraculous wilderness of gestation is my new frontier. I'm looking ahead, gathering provisions. I think I'm becoming a mother.

The woman's name was Anna and this is her second pregnancy; she lost her first child last year to a rare disease. She had sadness in her eyes for the one she lost, but excitement in her laugh for the one to come. I got choked up talking to her. She was inspiring and vulnerable, and I wanted to hug her and take care of her and marvel at her. I was a mess. She lost her child, and then summoned the faith to do it all over again. How do human beings do it?

May 18

Stayed up all night finishing a book review of a new Audre Lorde biography I agreed to write months ago. What a fascinating life. At one point she had a husband, two kids, and a wife—my kind of woman! But she also had major issues: a raging temper, self-absorption that wasn't easy on her kids or lovers. I am determined to live in a way that puts my baby first. I would rather not have a child than subject another human being to eking out an identity in the wake of unbridled narcissism.

But are narcissists aware of their narcissism? I could be going along la-di-da, thinking everything is fine, oblivious to how my choices are impacting my child. I have to rely on Glen to keep me on track. Last night he told me for the umpteenth time that being a parent is easy if you put the needs of the children first. If we can figure out what is best for them and do that, he says, we'll be okay.

May 19

Super-depressed and nauseated today. Can't eat. Keep having sick fantasies that the baby is going to be deformed and Glen is going to have a freak accident and leave me to raise the baby alone. I spent hours looking at the listings the realtor sent over. Two-bedroom unrenovated houses for a million dollars. My deformed child and I are going to live in a shack.

Definitely depression. I'll be puttering away, feeling fine about it all, and then, wham! The undertow.

May 20

Long day. Depressed in the morning, but managed to eke out an hour or so of writing. I forgot the second thing depression takes from me: productivity.

Had lunch with a writer friend in the afternoon. While we were waiting for our udon, Tina told me about her pregnancy: She was twenty-one, alone, and barely out of foster care. She ate M&M's all day and taught herself how to be a parent by reading Dr. Spock. She said she was too proud and too angry to say she needed help and ended up alone and depressed.

I am not sure why, given what she told me, but I asked if she wanted another child. She said absolutely not, no, never. She had preeclampsia, a pelvic cavity not big enough for the baby, and a C-section. She was left with stretch marks all over her body and a baby who at six weeks had to have an operation because he wouldn't stop projectile vomiting.

I got it, but as she was talking I kept thinking about her son, Mark. He is absolutely gorgeous. Smart and athletic. Sweet. The last time I saw him, he was wearing khakis and a white sweater and looked like a movie star. He hugged his mom and kissed her on the cheek. It just doesn't seem possible that he could be the result of such a hideous experience, and yet there it is: the contradiction at the core of the whole endeavor.

A documentary on celibacy was on a few nights ago, and on it, a psychiatrist talked about the urge to procreate and how it is the strongest human urge, stronger even than the urge to eat. That will to multiply—the sheer force of it leaves me speechless. Take this one in my belly. He (or she) is determined to be here. I can feel the force of his being. It's as if he has something to do here and just wants to arrive and grow up so he can get to it. *He's* not ambivalent at all.

On the way home, I stopped by my mother's house and shook my head as she dismissed my concerns about money and affordable housing for the baby. *Easy for her to say,* I thought. She's got four huge, beautiful houses. I had to remind her that when she was pregnant with me, my father had already bought their house and was supporting her utterly and completely, an option never presented to me, as a baby feminist, as feasible. Letting a man support me while I nest and think positive thoughts, that is.

Anyway.

Leaving her house, I was compelled to do a little retail therapy. Of course, the whole time I was shopping I was thinking that once the baby comes I will never shop again because I will have to pay for diapers and child care and car seats and bottles and blankets.

The thought was like walking into an airplane propeller.

May 21

Went to see Marie. She agrees with Glen that because of the hereditary predisposition to pregnancy-related depression (and because of the mood swings, three-hour crying spells, and thoughts so horrible I feel ashamed to even write them down), I should consider increasing the dose of my antidepressant. Even though I troll the Internet almost every night looking for articles on the impact of antidepressants on babies, I felt relief just hearing her say the words.

I know that between the two of us, the baby is the most vulnerable right now and I need to do everything I can to protect her, but I have to take care of myself, too. I feel selfish and guilty, but also self-aware and proud. I haven't succumbed to the cultural pressure to sacrifice my hard-won sanity if it isn't absolutely necessary. I'm still a whole human being with needs. I'm an equal partner in this baby equation.

I'm still agonizing over untold possibilities, but I feel fortunate to live at a time when depression is recognized as a treatable illness rather than, say, a religious or criminal defect. At least a few people understand that the choice I'm making isn't frivolous, it's necessary.

May 23

Dreamed last night about my ex-boyfriend Andrew, but I think I was really dreaming about all of the guys I have loved but didn't have children with. In the dream, Andrew and I were driving down a narrow road. It was overcast. Huge limestone churches and tiny houses covered with thatch came in and out of focus out the window. I was talking, and kept touching Andrew's hand as he moved the gear stick. He nodded and looked at me at all the right moments, but responded to me in Russian. Flowery, emphatic, lightning-fast Russian. I thought to myself that I must know how to speak his language and I cycled through all of the languages I know bits and pieces of, but could find no Russian. It dawned on me that we had no way to communicate, and that we had been this way for a very, very long time. I didn't flinch, and calmly kept stroking Andrew's hand, but I thought to myself that our relationship was over, and that everything was about to change.

This must have something to do with the e-mail I got from Andrew a few days ago. I have been thinking so much about our five-year relationship and what went wrong. The last time I saw him, he was living in Japan and teaching English. I traveled twenty hours to visit him, and after four days of wandering through temples in Kyoto and two days on a ferry to Shikoku, we had a huge, melodramatic fight complete with screaming and slamming doors and walking out of apartments in the middle of the night.

I ended up fleeing back to Narita airport in Tokyo in a taxi that cost three hundred dollars, driven by an officious man wearing white gloves and a little black cap. I didn't understand a word he said, but every ten minutes he would catch my eye in the rearview mirror and say, Narita? And I would look back at him and say, Yes, Narita. And he would say, Okay.

I can't remember what Andrew and I fought about, but I have missed knowing, over these last ten years, whether he is alive or dead, happy or miserable. Within forty-eight hours of Googling him, I was staring at photos of his beautiful wife and daughter. They are living in Hawaii; Andrew is weeks away from his Ph.D. In his note he sounded the same. Same dry British-American wit, same Sephardic warmth. I told him about the baby and he congratulated me. He said he always knew I would be a wonderful mother.

I woke up this morning feeling the distance between my life now and all the people I still love but no longer know. After a lifetime filled with a seemingly endless array of choices, I'm somewhat stunned to find myself making such a definitive one. It's thrilling to be opening the door to a new life with Glen, but terrifying to be shutting all the other doors to all the other lives. A part of me wants to leave an escape route open, some ember from an old flame smoldering, just in case. But another part says, No, this is it, you have a child to think about now, and turns away.

Three

LIKE MANY WOMEN MY AGE, I spent a good deal of time and energy trying not to have a baby. I may be speaking too broadly here, but I don't think so. Mine is the first generation of women to grow up thinking of children as optional, a project that might pan out to be one of many worthwhile experiences in life, but also might not. We learned that children were not to be pursued at the expense of anything else. A graduate degree in economics, for example, or a life of renunciation, devoted to a Hindu mystic. To live life as one long series of adventures in "sexual freedom" could be added to the list, along with becoming president, or at least secretary of state.

I don't remember exactly how these ideas were transmitted, but that I imbibed them is unquestionable. It must have had something to do with my mother being a cultural icon, and the private carry-over of her public insistence that even one child could, if not managed properly, erode one's hard-won independence. In an oft-quoted essay she wrote as a young mother, she remembers her mother's admonition to have a second child as uncharacteristically bad advice. In a poem written around the same time, she compares me to various calamities that struck and impeded the lives of other women writers. Virginia Woolf was mentally ill and the Brontës died prematurely. My mother has me, whom she lists as a delightful distraction, but by context and comparison, it's clear I was a calamity just the same.

The effect of living with my mother's ambivalence about the role of children in a woman's life, the role of *me* in her life, could not bode well having my own. Ambivalence itself is rarely positive. Ambivalence about one's offspring is a horrific kind of torture for all involved. It affects me to this day, stealing my certitude at critical moments. I have sat with others and said, Well, of course my mother loves me. But in the very next moment I will purse my lips and squint my eyes and tilt my head back and remember all of the indices of ambivalence, and the thought will arise with an even greater clarity: or maybe she does not.

People who cannot conceive of parental ambivalence have a very difficult time understanding this, and write it off as the confusion and ingratitude of children. But this is the price of ambivalence over a lifetime: It doesn't go away. It seeps into otherwise healthy tissue and tinges it with seeds of pathology. Does my mother love me unconditionally? Will it be possible to love my own child this way?

There was also the veiled competition that throbbed between my mother, an extremely driven artist determined to be successful on her own terms in a decidedly antagonistic world, and my step-mother, an equally educated woman who, more than anything else, wanted to give birth to and raise five children. I can't say that these two did not get along, because in order for this to be true they would have had to spend time with each other, and they only met four times in thirty years. But their respective choices, the extremely divergent ways they constructed and displayed their femininity, loomed large in my mind. So large that the tension between the two of them as individuals, typical stepmother–birth mother tensions, with the added challenges of being from different races and socioeconomic backgrounds, was transformed in my psyche as a tension between ways of being a woman.

Because these things are impressed upon us often before we realize we have a mind that can be impressed upon, I instinctively felt that I must be loyal to my mother's version. This meant maintaining my autonomy at all costs. To stop working and raise children, to be weighed down with tots like so many anvils around my neck, none of these were acceptable. They smelled of betrayal and a lack of appreciation for the progress made on behalf of women's liberation. Worse, they suggested a kind of ignorance about the truth of the gendered world, which was that unless women refuse, their children would enslave them. Which was that the myth of blissful motherhood was just that, a myth, and the reality was much more banal.

The only problem with this program was my stepmother. She wasn't especially well known or respected in her field, and she too, as a stepmother, had her share of ambivalence about being in a relationship with me. But my stepmother brought maternal enthusiasm and predictability to my life. She was enthusiastic about children in general and being a parent specifically, and predictable in that I could count on her to be the neurotic and intrusive maternal figure that Jewish mothers are often characterized as being. While my own mother could be counted on to recommend a life-changing book and to take me to a fascinating but remote village in Indonesia, my stepmother could be counted on to keep the refrigerator stocked with low-fat but tasty food, and to bring at least one camera to all events at which any of her children were to be featured.

Because divorce was not yet the exhausted psychological terrain it is today, there were no adults in my life who had the wherewithal to identify my dilemma and help me navigate it. There was no one who said to me, the way we now say to kids who are mixed race or bi-religious or have two daddies, Isn't it wonderful that you have these two role models and they are both so different! No one said over and over again (because that's how many times it takes) or even once, When you grow up you can embrace motherhood wholeheartedly and still accomplish great things. It seems absurdly obvious now, but growing up, I swear, I could not fathom it.

I dealt with the impossibility of my predicament by pretending it didn't exist. I made the requisite strides toward personal fulfillment through professional achievement, telling myself that I would think about having a baby when the time was right. Because I believed that there would be several if not dozens of other possible partners, at twenty I abandoned the first man with whom I could actually imagine having children, and didn't make another serious attempt until ten years later.

At the time, I felt relieved. Then I felt sad and despondent. Then I began to dream that my breasts were being chopped off with a huge machete. Constantly. Every day. By the time I got to therapy, I had seen my breasts chopped off at least ten thousand times. By the time I realized, also in therapy, that it was my own hand on the knife, I was already deep into another relationship, infusing it with the same ambivalence. Did I want a husband, children? Did

I want to be free and empowered to do whatever I wanted? Was the latter just a ruse to sabotage the former?

The ambivalence reared its head, this time with a slightly different presentation. I began to tell people hesitantly, Yes, I do want kids, but I am afraid. Afraid? the person or persons would reply. Of what? Hurting them, I would say. And then they might look at me with surprise or shock or understanding, and I would feel a twinge of shame and sadness, and then we would go on talking about something else, as if nothing was wrong or odd or out of the ordinary whatsoever.

Although it may have been risky, I wish someone had told me right away and with great emphasis, It is okay to worry, but don't by any means let it keep you from having a child! Instead of telling me that I had plenty of time, or that I should adopt because the world is full of needy children, someone should have sat me down, looked me right in the eye, and told me not to let anything keep me from the experience. Trust me, they could have said, barring disease, famine, and the potential for life-threatening violence or financial ruin, no matter what your trepidation, just do it.

They could have shared some version of what my gynecologist told me fifteen years later: "I've delivered thousands of babies, and as a rule, women don't regret having children, they regret not having them."

It is shocking to think that not one person suggested that my fear of hurting my children might really have been a fear of growing up and following my own (not my mother's) belief system.

Because the fact is that until you become a mother, you're a daughter. The fact is that when you almost die so that someone else can live, you become a much larger human being. The fact is that none of the ideas we've gleaned about motherhood from the mothers we know and the mothers we watch on TV mean anything at all because motherhood is in the doing, not the thinking about. Motherhood is brand-new every time; motherhood is full of possibility. Just like when John and Yoko said "War Is Over." Motherhood Is Free.

If you want it.

May 24

Spoke with my artist friend Sarah today. She gets the prize for the most foot-in-mouth response: You're pregnant? Oh my God, congratulations! My friend just had a miscarriage.

After an awkward pause, I said, Yeah, well, I'm not going to be having one of those, thank you very much, and then we both cracked up.

I've been getting e-mails from all over and they are all so beautiful and supportive. Yesterday Rikke wrote that I shouldn't worry, there is a reason it takes nine months to give birth: That's how long it takes for the reality of it to set in.

May 26

We got to Mendocino last night to find that a mouse has eaten through all of my clothes. I came up to bed and found one arm of my black sweater, chewed off as perfectly as a piece cut from a dress pattern, lying on the floor. We've got to get a cat. Or call Terminix.

On the way up from the city, Glen and I got into a huge argument about the birth and who will attend. My fantasy is that everyone I know and love will climb into the hot tub-cum-birthing pool with me. They will rub my legs and massage lavender essential oil into my scalp. Those who don't want to be in the water, or need a break from the festivities, will take shifts operating the iPod, or cooking. Every half hour I will be offered a fresh serving of pasta with garlic and oil, or organic chocolate cake. When the baby is born, everyone will say a blessing from a different spiritual tradition before we cut the cord.

Glen thinks my polytheistic fiesta theme is unrealistic and unsafe and doesn't honor the primacy of our relationship. He said he refused to be a part of a birth that was more than five miles from a hospital. He kept asking where we, as a couple, fit into my vision. Is there anything that is only for us? he wanted to know. Had I considered the impact that sharing such a major event will have on our intimacy as a couple? And what if something goes wrong? Do we really want that many people in the middle of such a critical moment?

He made some good points, but I wasn't ready to hear them. Instead I launched into a tirade about how it is *my* birth experience, and it should be however *I* want it to be, and how *dare* he even ask about *us*. For God's sake, I yelled, we have the rest of our lives to be together, why on earth should we be so *precious* and *controlling* about the birth? And anyway, I yelled, *studies show* that women surrounded by family and friends have shorter, *easier* labors. To which Glen replied, Well, that's great, but have there been any *studies* on the *divorce rates* for those women?

After a few minutes of strained silence, I had a flash of the baby and how arguments like these might frighten him or her, if they don't already. I thought about something Glen and I have talked a lot about: not arguing, and prioritizing peace between us over whatever ideas our intellects have gotten hooked on. I never want ideology or "being right" to take precedence over loving one another and being a family. There's just too much to lose. The baby's mental health and Glen himself are just a couple of things that come to mind.

And so I am rethinking the birth plan, and telling the little voice that wants everything her way that she has to be open. You're not alone anymore, I keep telling her. And that's a good thing. Yeah, right, she says, and turns her face the other way.

Before we went to bed, we talked about names. I've been calling the baby Milarepa, after a Buddhist ascetic who tamed both human beings and animals by singing to them.

Maybe we should name the cat Milarepa. Or the mouse.

May 28

Carl came over to look at the water heater this morning. Turns out it is "pretty ancient," and mineral deposits have built up inside the tank, taking up all the room where the hot water should go. He said it's a fire hazard, and that by the way, when he was looking at the heater he noticed that the main supporting beams under the bathhouse also need replacing. This last alert evoked a gruesome image of the building collapsing and pitching the baby and me out of the bathtub and into a patch of poison ivy.

After he left, I did two phone interviews from last week that Leslie, my publicist, rescheduled for today. The first interviewer was a young woman from Detroit who "loved" the latest collection of essays I've edited, *What Makes a Man: 22 Writers Imagine the Future.* She asked questions about the contributors, the importance of looking critically at masculinity, and the relationship between this book and *To Be Real: Telling the Truth and Changing the Face of Feminism,* an anthology about Third Wave feminism I edited ten years ago.

The second interviewer was an ex-Marine who claimed that male aggression is biological, that men who don't believe this are gay, and that I am offending our armed forces by questioning male aggression while our country is at war. When I told him that we probably had more in common than he thought, he said that no, he didn't think so. I said, Well, I am going to bet that we both want peace, and that neither of us wants our children to be killed in war. He said that war is necessary for democracy, and that he would be willing to sacrifice his child for the preservation of the American way of life.

He might be right about all of it, but when he said he'd be willing to sacrifice his child, a huge wave of exhaustion came over me. I felt that if I didn't lie down that very second, I might collapse. I exited as politely as I could, made for the kitchen, and scarfed the entire pot of soup Glen made last night. Then I climbed up the little ladder to bed and fell asleep.

It's now four in the morning. I have been sleeping for almost ten hours, but I still have the voice of the interviewer in my head. For what would I be willing to sacrifice my child?

June 1

Arrived at JFK in New York for the first time with baby on board. Everything was different because now all I can see are the women with babies. Were they always here? I am obsessed with how they move. Are they alone or do they have help? What kind of stroller are they pushing? Do they have a purse *and* a diaper bag? Cute or sensible shoes? Do cabdrivers do anything special to make it easier for them? Do they look happier than the childless women teetering by in high-heeled Manolos?

Now at my father's house on the Upper East Side, getting ready for the long drive tomorrow to see Solomon, the now fourteen-year-old young man I've been helping to raise since he was eight, at boarding school. Since his mother and I broke up, we've been trading off visiting days. I get the two days before his graduation from ninth grade, she gets actual graduation and the day after.

In what seems to be yet another manifestation of my ambivalence affliction, I can't figure out if I should tell Sol about the baby. I remember how abandoned I felt when my stepmother told me she was going to have her own biological child. The least I can do is spare him those feelings during a time that's supposed to be all about him and his accomplishments. On the other hand, I am pretty sure I'm showing, and I don't want him to figure it out and have to ask.

Pondering this, I feel an awful conflagration of elation and dread. I think I already love this little being inside of me more than I've ever loved anyone. How will this affect this person I consider to be, in many ways, my first child, the son I didn't give birth to but whom I adore nonetheless?

June 2

Arrived in Lake Placid after a long drive out of the city. I hung out with Solomon at his school for the evening, eating and talking to his housemates and a few other parents who came up early for graduation. I heard about miles hiked, potatoes harvested, accidents sustained while snowboarding, and "hook-ups." I was regaled with a *very* graphic description of the three a.m. birth of a lamb, and told that I am one of the coolest parents because I am young and wear "cool" clothes.

I like these kids. Over the last couple of years, I've watched them give presentations in their biology and Spanish classes, and even take stabs at improv. I've talked to their parents and grandparents, and heard their personal stories, many of them difficult. I am always in awe of how happy they seem in this environment. How the intimate, back-to-the-land, child-centered learning philosophy brings out their shiny, forceful natures.

Now that I am pregnant, I can't help but wonder if this place had something to do with it. There's a utopic feeling here, kids and adults together in the wilderness, planting, harvesting, learning, playing. I've liked knowing Sol is here, safe through the trials of 9/11 and largely unaware of its aftermath. Driving back to the hotel, I thought, Well, if I sink into a depression that threatens to damage my child, or if I buckle under the pressure of balancing the demands of work with the constant labor of motherhood, or if Glen leaves me and never wants to see me or his child again and I'm devastated, there's always boarding school. It sounds awful, but the thought was infinitely reassuring.

I told Sol about the baby within the first hour, after I caught him checking out my waistline. He was excited and immediately told his favorite houseparent, who, in addition to being a total Macintosh devotee, is a caring, gentle guy. I took his excitement as a sign that I haven't wrecked his graduation moment, and that the whole biological, nonbiological sibling thing just might work out.

June 3

I drove over to the school and spent the whole day. I asked Sol to take me to his favorite places on campus, the places he will miss the most. He took me on a trail through the woods to an old tree house, and then I followed him to the other side of the campus, to the tents around the lake. We stood there for a few minutes, getting lost in the shimmering water and wide-open sky.

Solomon will stay with me tonight at the hotel, and in the morning I will take him back to school and say goodbye. I am sad I will miss his departure speech, but I believe this way is best for everyone. In addition to the other complex dynamics of the day, including the presence of Solomon's biological father whom I don't really know, I feel protective of the baby. I don't want him or her to, for one second, get caught up in the emotional aftermath of the separation from Solomon's mother I've worked so hard to put behind me.

When I asked Solomon how he felt about the split schedule, he gave me his usual "Why are you always asking me how I *feel?*" look, and said it was fine.

I'm afraid that's the best I can do and, for once, I can live with that.

June 4

I love New York: the movement, the fashion, the dynamism. The heady mix of high and low. It's like a drug. Whenever I visit, I have to brace myself for the wave of ambivalence about California that washes over me. I miss the endless IV drip of films, performances, plays, and shopping. Food delivery of any kind at any time. Tasti D-Lite. Fortunately, I've been on this roller coaster enough times to know that in another forty-eight hours I'll start getting tired and missing the more reasonable rate of stimulation of the other coast. In seventy-two hours I will be pining for home.

I am happy to report that it's a little easier to feel good about my decision now that I've got the tot to think about. I want the baby to know New York so intimately that it loses its power to frighten and overwhelm. So intimately that she can harness the power of it for her own dreams. I owe her that. But fighting it out with a stroller on the subway? I just don't see it.

June 5

I have decided to stop using "her" and "she." Yes, I want to counter all of those years of the masculine pronoun standing in for all of humanity, but I really, really know in my heart that I am having a boy. It's the most obvious thing in the world to me. I refuse to allow my political beliefs to trump my intuition because that was the point of all of those political beliefs, wasn't it? To be able to trust our intuition?

June 6

My sister and stepmother took me shopping today for more maternity clothes. My sister took on the role of personal shopper, perusing the racks, and my stepmother was the voice of reason.

It was like being back in junior high, in a good way, until we split up and I tried to brave "the biggest maternity department in the city" by myself. All I got there was a big headache and another crashing wave of depression. Was it the J.Lo blaring through the store's speakers, the haggard-looking mothers being dragged around by whiny, unruly kids, or the upbeat, colorful display of tees I couldn't fit into juxtaposed against maternity wear that looked like it belonged on Dora the Explorer? Hmmm, let me think.

I got so freaked out walking around the store, I had to call Glen just to get my bearings. I know he must have thought I was losing it because I kept saying, Is this what's going to happen to me? Am I going to be trapped behind a stroller for the rest of my life, at the beck and call of some badly behaved toddler screaming for his sippy cup? And will I be wearing beige chinos and an oversized T-shirt with a company logo on it? And will I look and be so tired that I won't even care?

It reminded me of the *Sex and the City* episode when Miranda volunteers to frost her ex-boyfriend's new girlfriend's birthday cupcakes, and she calls Carrie in tears. Carrie's like, Why are you doing that? and Miranda kind of flops around, not knowing what to say. Then Carrie gets serious and tells Miranda to step away from the cupcakes.

After trying to talk me down three or four different ways, Glen finally told me to get out of the store. And even though he was three thousand miles away, and just a bunch of little sound waves coming through a piece of plastic, I did.

June 7

Spent a few hours today having my portrait taken by Marion Ettlinger, who has taken so many amazing author photos. She took the image of Lucy Grealy I like so much, with the bird on her shoulder, and the stunning portrait of Jhumpa Lahiri. Marion was great, warm but not overly so. We talked, but her eyes did most of the work, quietly taking me in. Her studio felt like a writer's study in Paris circa 1920, very Anaïs Nin and Henry Miller, all dark velvet chaises and antique wooden side tables, thirty-five-millimeter cameras and natural light.

While she was shooting, we talked about getting married. She loves her guy and wants to tie the knot, but feels she'd be selling out her feminist roots. I laughed and said, It's official, female ambivalence has reached an all-time high, it's an epidemic! I told her about how long I've wanted a baby and how scared I am. I told her that the only way I've been able to do it has been to choose my persistent, irrational, very human yearnings for closeness with other human beings over admittedly valuable feminist ideology that wasn't born of my own experience. I asked, If the relationship is healthy, is there ever a reason to let ideology keep us from committing more deeply to the people we love?

I can't say I have the answer, but I do think it's a legitimate question.

When we were done, I headed downtown to my friend Trajal's dance performance. Afterward, a bunch of us went to dinner, where the baby and his name were the main topics of conversation. The response to "Milarepa" was lukewarm, but people liked "Tenzin," after the Dalai Lama, which I've been throwing around for the last few weeks.

Tenzin Walker, our playwright friend Brooke said, that's strong. Trajal took to it right away, and started to include Tenzin in all our future plans. Well, when Tenzin is born, we'll have to have a party, and, I can't wait to go to Paris with Tenzin.

Paris with Tenzin!

I felt like the belle of the ball. Even though it was Trajal's night, being pregnant makes every night my night. Not long ago I heard Dr. Christiane Northrup speaking about yin wisdom, and how the egg waiting for the sperm is full of it. The egg just calls out to the sperm and then waits, knowing the whole school is going to come calling. I feel like that. For the first time in my life, being is effortless. My job is to sit and glow. All I have to do is wait and the whole world, the whole big life experience, is going to come and land right at my feet.

Tenzin Walker!

June 8

Met with John Vaughn today for lunch. He's directing a project for the Twenty-First Century Foundation called the Black Men and Boys Initiative, focusing on the status of African-American men in our culture and what can be done to change it. The statistics are disheartening. Forty percent of African-American men drop out of high school. One in every four is incarcerated. I can't help but think of the assassinations of Martin Luther King, Jr., Medgar Evers, and Malcolm X. The dissolution of the Panthers through COINTELPRO. The marginalization of African-American men in every segment of American culture but hip-hop, jazz, and sports. How few African-American men I see at universities where I speak, supermarkets where I shop, restaurants where I eat. How rarely I see an African-American man on a plane.

Because they are so rare, I know most of the African-American men succeeding in corporate America. Richard Parsons at Time Warner, Kenneth Chenault at American Express. Russell Simmons, important because he has managed to make his millions without wearing a suit and tie, without forfeiting ownership, and without becoming unrecognizable to the people he grew up with, or to himself.

It is as if, in response to the leadership African-American men have displayed, they have been targeted for annihilation, or at least total subordination. It is as if, in response, African-American men have chosen to keep their intellects undercover, or not to develop them at all. Flipping through channels late at night and searching the shelves at the bookstore, I can't believe the glaring absence of African-American intellectualism. But being a brilliant black man can be dangerous, can put you in the crosshairs.

There are the academic superstars: Cornel West and Henry Louis Gates. Michael Eric Dyson. Across the Atlantic, Paul Gilroy. But where is the W.E.B. DuBois, the Frederick Douglass, the Dr. King of our time? The Bayard Rustin and James Baldwin? What happened to credible voices having the power to elucidate, to inspire and inform masses of people? How is it possible that so much of this work of social uplift is left to rap artists who have just barely escaped gangsterism? How is it possible that the African-American intelligentsia seems to have evaporated into the corporate media conglomerate, rarely if ever to be seen or heard providing cogent commentary on the state of affairs? Where are the translators, the people who deconstruct the news to the populace?

Listening to John, I got the feeling they are all in jail. And then I thought, *If I have a boy, how on earth will I protect him?*

June 9

Went to a screening of Spike Lee's film about a man who impregnates lesbians to make ends meet after being fired from a lucrative biotech job. I have to give it to Spike: He takes risks. The film was a little messy, but I don't think people appreciate how far Spike took the discussion within a conservative mainstream context that doesn't want to look at the possible obsolescence of the adult male. Reduced to sperm donors for rich, sexy lesbians? Come on, how easy could that have been to get funded?

I especially liked the scenes in which our hero feels objectified, used, and demoralized during and after sex, a trope usually reserved for women on-screen. It takes a lot of courage to reveal that men have these same anxieties. As they lose a sense of power and control at work and in their personal relationships, their psyches struggle to make the adjustment. I also found myself identifying with the women's intense quest for motherhood, and I appreciated how our hero ultimately partners with two of the women he has impregnated.

It was good to see people I haven't seen in years. Everyone patted my growing belly and seemed genuinely excited for me. Of course I had to pee like a million times and was sweating like I had my own personal sprinkler system hidden beneath my clothes. Have I documented that new side effect? That I get these raging hormonal surges that make me hot and flushed, and dripping with perspiration? It's quite attractive.

Went out to dinner with friends afterward, and then walked sixty blocks back to the apartment. I must be feeling better because my energy is way up and my brain seems to be clear and firing for the first time in weeks. Maybe, just maybe, I am coming out of this damn first trimester into what is supposed to be the fun part. I feel calmer, back to myself, not quite so hysterical and on edge.

Or maybe it's just New York. And the extra dose of the antidepressant Marie prescribed back in San Francisco.

Either way, I talked to Glen as I walked, my boots clicking against the filthy New York pavement, smiling and imagining walking the same city streets with him and the baby.

June 14

Heartbeat! Oh my God. The most outrageous thing I have ever heard. I went in for my second prenatal with Dr. Lowen and, as usual, it was in and out, but the "in" included hearing my baby's heartbeat. Dr. Lowen was completely unimpressed, and she's allowed, considering she hears a gajillion baby heartbeats a day. But I was completely, totally, stupendously overwhelmed. I was floating all over the office. It was all I could do to keep myself from grabbing the Doppler ultrasound and holding it to my stomach for hours.

I am happy to report that the heartbeat is absolutely perfect. Strong, fast, well paced. I took this as another sign that I really do have a baby inside of me. This isn't some vast conspiracy to trick me into believing something that isn't true. In six more months, a real live baby is going to come out of my body and make me a mother. I know, I know, it sounds crazy. But it's true.

To add to my growing distaste for the whole doctor vibe, on my way out the receptionist handed me my "complimentary" diaper bag. It was full of formula samples and coupons for several other baby products. I could take the appreciative and noncynical tack, but I can't believe doctors allow themselves to be the middlemen and -women for these companies. In the intimacy of my doctor's office, where I am, by design, vulnerable and open to her suggestion, seeking it even, I am being marketed to. Am I being too sensitive? It's like commercials at the movies times a hundred.

When I gave the bag back to the nurse, declining politely, she looked at me like I was crazy. Just keep it, she said, you might need it. I just put it on the counter. I don't think so, but thank you so much. Then I worried for an hour that I had come across as an arrogant, ungrateful bitch.

Glen continues to think I should find another OB. He was over Dr. Lowen when we went in for the fertility consultation and she made a remark about men getting bent out of shape when women, "who do so much," ask them to "do a little thing like take a motility test." He felt the remark was insulting, considering all he does, and insensitive, considering the societal mandate that "real men" be virile in the same way that "real women" should be fertile. Even though it isn't a big issue for him, he thinks it is callous for a doctor to miss the fact that motility can be a sore spot for men.

He's right, of course. He totally clocked one of those gynic moments that make me cringe. Moments in which women intent upon "claiming their power" do or say things that belittle the men they say they love.

I mostly agree with Glen about finding another doctor, but the idea of starting the search makes me want to go take a nap. I have been seeing Dr. Lowen for a few years and, I tell Glen with a grin, she's got biracial kids. Glen has accused me of being a sucker for the parents of mixed-race kids more than once. I project noble qualities onto them and make excuses for their bad behavior.

Glen shakes his head. He's not happy that the criteria for staying with the gynecologist who might deliver our baby is her biracial children, but he doesn't revisit the highly contentious discussion we've been having lately about how all of the big baby decisions seem to be made exclusively by me, and I couldn't be more grateful for the respite.

June 22

Had a long, intense discussion with my lobbyist friend Rachel about how many women rely on the samples given to them by their obstetricians because, unlike most developed nations, and even some not-so-developed nations, America has no social support system to speak of for new parents. Paid parental leave, which can be up to two years in countries like Sweden and Denmark and divided between two parents, is virtually nonexistent here, with American women getting only six weeks, if they're lucky. High-quality public child care for preschool-aged children is also the norm in countries like France, but completely unavailable in the United States, forcing new parents to work long hours to even have a shot at affording excellent child care.

It's hard to understand why our country, one of the wealthiest in the world, seems to care so little about its children. Even from a purely capitalist point of view, you would think that well-looked-after, well-educated children would ensure a competent workforce and stable populace. And studies show that women are able to be more productive with this kind of support, so it's not like we'd lose half the GDP. Rachel thinks it has to do with the low expectations of families in America. Women have been getting six weeks to three months for so long it seems normal, an unquestionable standard.

But I think it also has to do with our cultural ambivalence about the role of biology in women's lives, and how it has been used to suppress and control women. For generations, women were portrayed as the weaker sex, more emotional and less physically capable than men, and so biologically unsuited for positions of power. In response to this disempowering narrative, women said no, we aren't inherently anything at all. Shaped by culture and not biology, we can be anything we want to be. Tactically, this was a smart move. By maintaining that women are inherently the same as men, and so deserving of equal treatment, we gained some access to what had been previously denied.

The problem is that men don't get "special treatment" when they have babies, so why should women? Which leaves infants in the arms of hired caregivers instead of their mothers. This strategy has also left women somewhat ambivalent about maternal desire. Is it a biological yearning that should be denied in the name of sameness and women's empowerment? The whole polemic puts women in the ridiculous position of wondering whether wanting a baby is proof that women actually *are* the weaker sex.

I think that parental, rather than maternity, leave is a good way of negotiating this point in the public sphere. We avoid the potentially divisive and ultimately unknowable question of whether women are fundamentally different from men by saying that both parents need and deserve to take care of their children. But what if we are fundamentally different? Before I got pregnant I would have vehemently rejected this idea. Now I'm not so sure. Now I might try a different tactical approach: Do men and women have to be the same to be treated equally?

I left Rachel's house thinking about what it really means to cut taxes in this country. It means that, among other things, the bond between parents and children is not supported with programs like extended parental leave, and children's psychosocial and intellectual development is neglected in the absence of excellent and affordable child care. It also means that many people can't afford to have children at all, let alone provide them with what they need to succeed.

In a country, a world, as rich as ours, this is unacceptable. Reflecting on what this process has meant to me already, in terms of experiencing what it means to be human, I can't help but feel that having children should be a right, not a privilege.

June 23

I met with my midwife Sonam again today. She tested my urine by having me pee on a stick that changed colors, took my temperature, measured my uterus, and listened to the baby's heartbeat with the Doppler, talking to me about baby stuff the whole time. She suggested I start doing prenatal yoga, gave me the names of a couple of teachers she likes, and told me to eat wild salmon and leafy greens. I told her that all I want to do is wander from room to room, have sex, eat, and sleep, and she laughed. That's okay, she said, but remember, labor is a marathon: You have to train. Shoot. You mean I can't just lounge around my boudoir for nine months?

We talked a little business, like what I think about the hospital where she has privileges being public and twenty to thirty minutes away. When I asked what she meant, exactly, by the public part, she said that the hospital is well equipped and has a great neonatal intensive care unit, but serves a very different population than the hospital I usually go to.

She said it's not one-thousand-percent spotless, either. It's an older building and hasn't been renovated. For the most part, the nurses are excellent and she loves her supervising doctor, but the best thing about the place is that she has full privileges there, which means she would be in charge of the birth unless something goes wrong.

What can I say? I wish the public and private hospitals weren't so different. I wish I didn't have to negotiate race and class just to have my baby. I'm going to visit and see how it feels, but I'm pretty sure I'd rather have Sonam deliver this baby in a lean-to than risk having an unnecessary C-section in some spotless shrine to the medical establishment.

At least I think I would.

June 28

Today I met June for lunch. We talked about our new creations: hers, a new publishing venture; mine, the little one growing in my belly. She told me she long ago decided not to have children. She said that several of her friends had children because they thought they should, only to realize too late that they didn't make the decision consciously. Where are they with it now? I wanted to know. They've got kids they don't want, she said, shaking her head.

Yikes.

When I asked more about her decision, she said she didn't feel emotionally able to take care of herself, let alone a defenseless child. Her body was too weak, having weathered a few major illnesses, and her energy too elusive. Her husband wanted kids, but when she asked if it was him or the culture that wanted them he conceded it was the culture. Then she brought her sister's kids home to prove her point. The kids exhausted both her and her husband.

I tried not to get judgmental about her choice. I tried to minimize the whole baby thing and just talk about work stuff, creative stuff, and the machinations of the publishing world. I tried not to gush about how long I have wanted a baby, and how miraculous it is to have another human being growing inside of me.

But it was damn near impossible.

Am I turning into a baby supremacist? One of those people who thinks a woman without a baby is like a fish without an ocean? Who thinks a woman without a baby may be stuck developmentally just shy of true adulthood forever? As June talked about her new office and staff, I thought about how much she's missing and how appalling it is that I can't tell her because the whole thing is so unbelievably primal and indescribable. I thought about how hooked human beings can get on external accomplishment, but how at the moment, the most dramatic and exciting changes of my life are happening inside and I have no desire to go back.

I know I'm setting myself up for some serious refutation, and it's all valid. My thoughts aren't rational. They're hormonal, irrational, psychopharmacological.

And so incredibly real.

Four

IT'S NOT THE SAME. I don't care how close you are to your adopted son or beloved stepdaughter, the love you have for your nonbiological child isn't the same as the love you have for your own flesh and blood.

It's different.

I met Solomon when he was seven and I was twenty-six. It was a sunny Los Angeles afternoon, and his mom, whom I had been dating for several weeks, was taking us to the beach. Solomon was wearing blue pants and carried several small plastic action figures. He was quiet and cautious, with intermittent bursts of chattiness. His parents were in the middle of a nasty divorce, and he reminded me of myself at his age, trying to figure out who to be after my parents sat me down and told me their marriage was over.

Within hours of meeting Solomon, I had projected a lifetime of alienation onto him, ascribing to him all the pain and confusion I felt after my parents ended their marriage. Within weeks I had fallen for him. I loved the way he took my hand when we were out in the city. The way he asked deep and seemingly bizarre questions like, When people die, do they remember who they've been? I loved that he thought he remembered being in his mother's womb and described it as warm, red, and mushy.

Before I even remotely knew whether a relationship with his mother was something I wanted, I dove into Solomon's life and began trying to create the positive post-divorce family I never had. Without thinking it through. Because I thought he needed me. Because I knew my inner seven-year-old needed me. And I had to save her. By saving him.

And so it began. The trips to the orthodontist and ophthalmologist, the monthly talks about schoolwork and conduct with the teachers of third, fourth, fifth, sixth, seventh, eighth, and then, finally, ninth grades. We had the obligatory struggles over homework, diet, and violent video games. I suffered the endless negotiation of the politics, socioeconomic and otherwise, of play dates. I hired helpers, bought and read books on teen sexuality, coalesced and counseled members of the extended family.

I did so much that friends wondered if I wasn't doing too much. I wasn't his *actual* mother, after all. And wasn't it true that if I did too much, I would enable her to do too little? What would happen if his mother and I should break up? Shouldn't I legally adopt him to protect my investment in our relationship? I understood their concerns, but my inner seven-year-old was undaunted. She wanted— no, *needed*—me to keep going.

I wasn't just reparenting myself, though. I was securing my position in the relationship. Love me, love my kid. That's what single parents say to potential lovers, partners, and spouses. Even when they don't utter the words, it's a running subtext. And don't we potential stepparents respond, if we believe we can make a genuine go of it, with our own subtext? We make dinner for three and watch *Princess Mononoke*. To the exciting new adult in our life we say: Your child is my child. To the adorable child before us we say: I think of you as my own. When we are in deep, and can see that the well-being of another human being is at stake and his ability to trust us *actually matters,* we look straight into his eyes and say: No matter what, I will never leave you.

At least that's what I said. It didn't occur to me that some people would predict a messy endgame and keep their distance. These people would have gone down the "Your child is my child" road with other lovers and friends, only to devastate some unsuspecting kid and get wiped out in the process. But I hadn't yet lost a child, and so I said all of the things I said because I meant them, and because I did not see a way to proceed in the relationship without meaning them. I said them because I had no idea what I was getting myself into. I said them because I was in love and didn't yet know how to think with any organ other than the one in my chest.

In the end I couldn't do it. I couldn't save me and I couldn't save him and I couldn't save her and I couldn't save us. It was an untenable situation and none of us had the skills to make it otherwise. The only thing I can say on our behalf is that we were in our twenties and early thirties and the relationship epitomized our developmental limitations. It was passionate and histrionic, fun and tragic, romantic and stupid.

Being young and coming from families that didn't stay together, we thought if we just loved long and hard enough we could destroy everything a thousand times and put it back together a thousand times, and then one day everything would fall into place. We thought it was like taking the train from the city to the beach. Concrete, traffic, pollution, and then a little less concrete and then a little less traffic and then a little less pollution and then voilà: the vast, undulating blue-green sea.

That was how I tried to hold my first child. As if one day all the arguing and moving about would be over and we would look at each other with the knowledge of all that came before and a deep appreciation for the peace we managed to create. After my separation from his mother, I still hold him that way. As if the cloudy day will pass. As if the distance and lost time will be eclipsed by a newfound togetherness. And it may. But it also may not, and there is very little I can do about it.

Already, months before his birth, I do not hold my second child this way. For starters, I no longer believe in the redemptive power of the calm after the storm. The wreckage on the shore does not disappear because the winds have moved on. When I think of my baby's soon-to-be-born face, full of wonder and unmarred by proximity to rage, I register the value of circumnavigating the storm, of moving inland where it is safe. Even though in the moment it may be more difficult, I now prefer to face the challenge rather than be left with the heartbreaking reality of irreparable damage.

There is also the simple fact that my second child can never be taken from me. We are bound through space and time in the beginningless beginning, that place of infinite mystery. We have met there, on that ground, in a meeting impossible to erase. Even when we are far from each other, we will each possess a fragment of that encounter, buried in the loamy dirt we call our separate selves. I am no longer inexperienced enough to diminish this connection.

There are other things. My stepmother told me a few days ago, again, that she feels I am one of her children, that she raised me as her own. I love her, and yes, in some ways I am one of her children, but in some ways I am not. It may be difficult to ascertain exactly where the line is between the two, but it is beyond question that the line exists. I can decide to care for my stepmother, for instance, but caring for my mother, no matter the state of our relationship, is not something about which I have a choice.

I find myself nodding as I read about a study that finds that children living with a stepmother receive a good deal less food, health care, and education than they would if they lived with their biological mother. It isn't something we are proud of, this preferencing of biological children, but if we ever want to close the gap, I do think it is something we need to be honest about. I left the conversation with my stepmother thinking, Yes, I would do anything for my first son, within reason. But I would do anything at all for my second child, without reason, without a doubt.

What does that mean for Solomon and me? Is our relationship stained by my confession that our bond isn't the same as the one I have with my biological child? Is it damaged if I say out loud that I love him differently?

I hope not. Solomon will always be my first child. He will forever be the one who inspired me to give endlessly and love selflessly, who showed me that I could become a parent after all. We, too, have a mysterious connection. We appeared in each other's lives when we needed each other the most.

In some ways I saved Solomon's life, and in some ways he saved mine. Without him, my first child, my second child may never have been conceived.

The fetus is now nearly 3 inches from crown to rump and weighs nearly an ounce—about half a banana. Its unique fingerprints are already in place. And when you poke your stomach gently and she feels it, your baby will start rooting— that is, act as if she's searching for a nipple.

June 29

Jesus.

All I can say is thank goodness I am taking the extra dose of meds. Two days ago I checked my e-mail to find a note from my mother threatening to send an attached statement to the editors of Salon.com in response to an interview I did a couple of weeks ago.

In a nutshell, she took offense to a section of my 2001 memoir, *Black, White, and Jewish,* that the interviewer reprinted, in which I wrote that my parents didn't protect or look out for me, but fed, watered, and encouraged me to grow. In the statement, she called me a liar, a thief (because when I was eight years old I took quarters from her purse during my parents' divorce), and a few other completely discrediting unmentionables. After posting back that unless she wanted out-and-out war, she should rethink her decision to send the letter, I went over to her house to find out what the hell was going on.

Never have I been so frightened by my own mother. She sat me down and called me, in addition to a liar and a thief, "someone who thinks she is a good person but really isn't," and someone who "would sell her own mother down the river." She told me that because I wasn't from the South and didn't have the full memory of slavery (read: I am half white), that I don't know what it feels like to be sold down the river, but that's how she felt after reading my book.

For the twenty-five-thousandth time, I apologized for telling my truth in a way that hurt her, and told her that I tried to protect her the best way I knew how. Then I asked whether she thought it was a little strange that I wrote about my struggle in an attempt to get her to take care of me, but here we were talking about how I should be taking care of her. Again.

She grew quite vicious. I told her repeatedly that I didn't think that what she was saying was very maternal. After two hours trying to convince her of the merits of my existence, I left the house shaking.

Glen was extremely upset: This is how she treats you, even when you're pregnant?

Between him and my father, who wrote my mother a letter saying that as parents it is their job to be proud of my accomplishments rather than undermine my livelihood, I managed to keep it relatively together, but it hasn't been easy.

I keep asking myself, If she's not able to put the needs of the baby first when he's inside of me, how is she going to do that when he's a walking, talking little boy?

June 30

Went with Glen to see his teacher, a high lama from Tibet who escaped by crossing the Himalayas on foot after the Chinese occupiers murdered his father. I always love going to see Khenpo, but given the last few days, it was even more special, like entering another dimension, a surreal world beyond the realm of explanation. He fed us huge beef ribs, the biggest I have ever seen, that he ate with a gigantic knife, expertly paring the meat away from the bone. Then we drank bone soup, which is supposed to be good for physical strength and heating up the body, but which made me want to throw up.

I can barely understand Khenpo when he talks, but Glen gets every word, and the two of them and another lama from Bhutan sat around telling jokes and laughing. I was so tired I had to go into another room to lie down, but I could hear them all the way upstairs and felt comforted, like I was in a pure land and the laughter of the dharma deities was my lullaby.

When we left, I asked Khenpo to bless the baby in my belly. He tapped my stomach and laughed. Bless the baby yourself! At first I was put off, then I realized it was his way of telling me I am as much a deity as he is, and that I shouldn't idealize him and deprecate myself. I have the power to bless my own baby.

July 5

I am at Alta Bates hospital in Berkeley, trying not to freak out. Last night I ate steak and spinach and salad and mint chocolate chip ice cream, and then got an awful pain in my stomach, like someone had taken a knife and stuck it into my gut. When I couldn't take it anymore, I called an ambulance and hobbled downstairs. By the time they got to the building, I was on the sidewalk on my hands and knees, doubled over with pain.

I crawled in the back and told the EMTs my blood type, doctor's name, and that I am four months into a normal pregnancy. The EMT, whom I expected to, I don't know, take my temperature or something, looked at me and said she didn't believe I was actually sick. She said if I was in as much pain as I said I was, I would be perspiring, or at least breathing heavily, and there were no signs of either, which made her skeptical.

I was like, um, are you kidding me? You think I just wanted to come and get into an ambulance for fun? And then she said, Well, ma'am, are you sure you aren't involved in a domestic dispute? My jaw dropped open almost to Chile. Then she changed course and asked if I had been taking drugs.

Fortunately, Glen drove up behind the ambulance at that moment, and I told the EMT to let me out. Unbelievably, she started saying all of this crazy stuff like they couldn't just let me go, I had to sign something and blah, blah, blah, which seemed absurd, considering she had just told me there was nothing wrong with me.

At the emergency room, a nice intern checked my vitals and then rolled in a portable ultrasound. After a few seconds of searching, I heard the baby's heartbeat and then the intern say the baby looks fine before bursting into uncontrollable sobs on the gurney. Talk about drama. I had been lying there thinking that I would rather die than lose the baby, and if I had to die to save him, that would be okay.

I didn't have to try to feel that way. There was no ambivalence, no inkling of possible relief at being let off the hook. I knew the truth of this as intimately as I knew my own name: My child must live. Period. End of story. Done.

Dr. Lowen arrived. The pain had subsided a little, and we were all close to letting it go as one of those crazy, bizarre moments in pregnancy. But just as the intern started to fill out the release form, the pain started again, stronger than ever, and that's when they started talking about a morphine drip for the pain. At that point I would have injected orange juice into my veins if they told me it would stop the pain, but morphine? I had visions of my baby emerging from the womb incoherent and addicted to opiates. As if reading my mind, Dr. Lowen said that it was relatively safe, and that sometimes during pregnancy you have to prioritize the mother's health. I nodded skeptically as the intern injected the needle in my arm.

I was admitted just as I fell into an opium-induced haze, and now here I am, the next morning, with a second IV in my arm and doctors coming in and out trying to figure out what's wrong with me. I keep suggesting to them that it's intestinal. I've been taking those giant iron tablets and eating ridiculous, absurd amounts of food. So far the internist and Dr. Lowen both say that the pain would be lower if it was intestinal. Whatever it is, I am really happy to have this drip.

July 6

The perinatologist came in today. She said that even though my blood and urine look normal, the location of the pain suggests a possible kidney infection. She recommended a baby-safe antibiotic. I will get it through the IV for the first two days and if the pain decreases, I can take the last dose at home. I asked her three times about the effects of the antibiotics on the baby, and if there were *any* studies that even hinted at adverse effects on the infant. Then I quizzed her on the morphine. She was very nice and assured me that both were okay. Not ideal, but okay. I asked her if she thought it might be intestinal. She didn't think so.

Glen came in just as she was leaving, with big bags of food. I dished it out on my pale green laminated tray, and poured us both some lemonade. I don't know what I would do without him. What do people do without other people? Why is it that so few people are competent in the caretaking department? I feel like the luckiest woman alive to have him sitting with me, going over the details of my conversation with the doctor as if his life depended on it, too.

I am concerned, but I'm also not so into being in the hospital. I have never felt comfortable with using Western medicine exclusively, which explains the small army of healers I have assembled over the years. I am especially not happy with the way the doctors dismiss my opinion of what might be wrong with me. Glen agrees it is hard to have faith in a place where people come in with one thing and then die from something else, but he thinks we should wait and see.

I want to call Marie, the M.D. homeopath, but (a) she's in Alaska, and (b) it might be dangerous to mix the systems. If Marie tells me to take something, then I will have to figure out how it interacts with what I am getting here; and if she has a different diagnosis, all of the doctors will be in disagreement, and I will be lying in my hospital bed betwixt and between, not sure what to do. Better to take this train to the end and then try the other if it doesn't kill me.

The only thing that makes staying bearable is the nurse coming in every two hours to check the baby. It's like having my own personal Doppler. I hear his quick little heartbeat, whoosh-whoosh, whoosh-whoosh, several times a day, and into the night. Fantastic.

July 8

The antibiotic has caused some kind of freak reaction. My white and red blood cell counts have plummeted, ditto for the hemoglobin. I now have acute, medication-induced anemia. The perinatologist came in, scratched her head, and I haven't seen her since. For some unknown reason, an infectious-disease doctor took her place, and she thinks we should discontinue the first baby-safe antibiotic and try a different one. As far as I can tell, there still isn't any indication in my blood tests that I have a kidney infection, but the pain hasn't let up and, well, it seems to be the only thing they can think of.

I asked the infectious-disease person if she thought it could be intestinal and she shook her head. She was very nice, too—slow, methodical, and seemingly knowledgeable. But when I asked her why she, an infectious-disease person, was put on my case, she didn't have a good answer, and that sounded alarm number 9,000.

Glen, exhausted from trying to get a good night's sleep on a coat rack disguised as a daybed, looked over at me after she left and asked what I thought. I said, I think all of these people are crazy and I should call Marie. And then a nurse walked in the door with the new medicine and started hooking it up to the IV.

July 9

Well, I have been here four days and don't have a diagnosis. The pain ebbed slightly today, but when one of the nurses opined that

I might not need the morphine drip, I panicked. It hasn't ebbed that much.

I have come to the conclusion that hospitals are not places for healing. The food is awful, the environment depressing, and the constant intrusion of the nurses makes resting almost impossible. I know I should be grateful that I have health care at all and insurance to pay for it, but it's hard when just as I am about to doze off, a nurse comes in to take my vitals.

Glen brought me some scarves to toss around the place, so I climbed out of bed this morning and walked around the room with my IV pole trailing behind me, "decorating." Now my bed has a beautiful pale green cloth over it, and the faded Seurat and Monet prints are all covered with gold and burgundy. I put the lilies Glen brought me on the little table next to the bed, and my books and laptop on the swiveling tabletop I'm using as a desk. Now I am sitting here typing in my favorite sea-green robe with pale pink flowers, and feeling a little more relaxed, like a part of home has been magically transported to the hospital.

A few minutes ago, my father and stepmother called. They were each on different phones in their apartment, asking questions and extracting new information. They're worried and want to know if they should come out. Judy says she can make chicken soup, and my father says he can just sit in the hospital with me. Neither of them can understand why my mother, who lives nearby, hasn't come to see me.

After our last encounter, I can't say I am in a hurry to see her. What I can say is that I have to focus on cultivating relationships with people who have the ability to love me the way I need to be loved.

Not just for my sake, but for the baby's.

July 10

I have got to get out of here. I am getting progressively worse, not better, and when I asked one of the doctors this morning how much this little visit is costing he couldn't say exactly, but somewhere in the ballpark of five to seven thousand dollars a day. Could that explain why there is no real hurry to release me? Is that cynical, or savvy?

A little while ago, a hematologist came in and told me he was surprised to see me looking so well because according to my blood counts, I should be close to unconscious. Then he started talking about the point at which we should talk about scheduling a transfusion. Transfusion? Glen and I nodded along with him, but the moment he left I told Glen that it was time to go. I've lost all faith in this place, and I feel strongly that I have to get out while I can. The anemia is acute, but I can treat that at home with beef, spinach, and even iron shots, if necessary. The pain has lessened somewhat, and if I can take two or three Tylenol every few hours, I think I can manage.

Our plan for getting out is to tell each and every doctor and nurse that comes in that I plan to leave tomorrow and that they should either tell me why that isn't possible, or start making preparations for me to leave.

We also called Marie, who said it sounded intestinal, especially in light of the fact that I have been taking the iron capsules (!!!). She instructed me to switch to a liquid diet and get the nurse to give me a laxative.

Glen went to get soup and I put in my request for a laxative, telling the nurse in the same breath that I am going home tomorrow. She said she would contact the doctor about the laxative and that she doubts very much that I will be able to leave tomorrow as there is no indication of it in my chart.

. . .

I JUST TALKED to the last doctor that had to be convinced and she finally, reluctantly, said I could leave. Not that I gave her any choice. *I am leaving tomorrow* has been my mantra since ten-thirty this morning, and as of about forty-five minutes ago, when the nurses confirmed that they finally got in touch with my doctors who are coming in to write my exit papers, it seems to be working.

At two o'clock, I still wasn't sure. One of the residents came in and told me she wasn't comfortable releasing me because my pain wasn't completely gone and my blood counts were so low. I was like, hello, I agree with you on how upsetting and strange this all, I just don't agree that staying is going to turn it around because if it was, wouldn't it have already? I stayed calm and didn't say anything because she started talking about giving me an AMA, which Glen explained is a slip that says I have left the hospital "against medical advice." I would have to sign it and clear the hospital of any liability should something happen to me after I leave.

The news that the only thing standing between the hospital and my release is a signature was a tremendous relief, and I was ready to sign right then and there. But after she left, Glen told me that sometimes insurance companies look unfavorably at patients who leave AMA, and could do anything from raise my premium to refuse to continue my insurance at the end of the term. I am aghast but so exhausted and weak that the most I can do is shake my head in disbelief. My will to ask a lot of questions about how that can be legally possible and whether or not most people know this is just gone.

Anyway, I don't want to go on a whole bender against the health-care system. I've been sick in places where there are no doctors and no hospitals, and that was beyond horrendous, but my goodness. It's like the old Gil Scott-Heron song about people walking on the moon while his sister is living in a tenement and getting bitten by rats.

Which brings me back to the matter at hand: Since I replaced the copious amounts of chicken and salad I was eating with soup, my stomach feels a thousand times better. Which is good because a nurse just told me that since I am leaving tomorrow, she is going to pull the morphine to see what happens overnight. I have become so dependent on the drip, I feel like a child being asked to hand over my blanket, pacifier, and favorite stuffed animal right after my mom has left the building. She's in the car, driving away, and the people taking care of me say, Okay, let's just have your blankie and your binky and your little piglet.

The strangest thing is that the doctors and nurses act like it's no big deal, like they're just pulling a sugar-water drip out of my arm and not one of the strongest opiates on the planet. I want to scream out, But I love my little white button! Can't I take it home with me? Which is the closest thing to addiction I've ever felt, if I don't count shoe shopping.

July 12

Home!

My levels are scary, way below normal. I went to see Marie, and she told me to eat boiled chicken, applesauce, something called congee, which is basically rice cooked over and over again until it is total mush, and vegetables overcooked 1950s style. She also told me to rest, and if possible to have people come and take care of me 24/7 for two weeks.

Argh. The idea of people taking care of me 24/7 for fourteen days was hard to wrap my mind around. Who could stop working, parenting, and maintaining their own lives to take care of me every hour, seven days a week? Do people even do that anymore in our crazy culture? What, then, do sick people do? They hire caregivers, obviously. But then you're living with a stranger, and I can't think of anything more stressful and depressing. Maybe people can come in shifts? Of course Glen says he can do it all and doesn't need help, but even though I joke about the imaginary cape he wears, he's not Superman.

Marie also told me to visualize a cute, normal, healthy baby, and a healthy remainder of my pregnancy. So that's what I've been doing all afternoon, while making congee and burning three pots of rice in the process.

July 17

I felt a little sorry for myself last night. I've been doing everything I am supposed to, but my labs are not improving as dramatically as they should. I've really taken a hit. Today my hematocrit, which is supposed to be between 36 and 50, is at 27. My hemoglobin is holding at 9. It should be between 12.5 and 17. The only good news is that my white blood cells, which were completely wiped out, are coming back, with a read today of 9.5, which is perfect.

I refused to let anemia hold me back, though. Today I:

- Watched three episodes of the sixth season of *Sex and the City*. I'm rooting for Miranda and Steve, even though that black Knicks doctor (Blair Underwood) is so sexy and it is nice to finally see an eligible, foxy black man on the show.

- Baked and ate an entire organic marble cake. *Delicious.* I see much baking in my future.
- Forced myself out of the house for a walk around the park. The sky was fiery red and purple, and there were lots of people out walking their dogs and riding bikes. I didn't get far, but it was heavenly to get some air.
- Pitched, to *Salon* and *Slate,* an interview with Spike Lee on his new movie, and did a little work on an essay for an anthology on guilt I agreed to write.

I am tired, but not dead.

July 19

Dinner at my mother's. She invited me with this loving, the-other-day-never-happened e-mail that of course sent me into a tizzy of indecision. What pregnant daughter doesn't want to be close to her mother? There should be a support group: Ambivalents Anonymous.

I asked Glen to come because I was truly, honestly, afraid of being alone with her. The last encounter was that disturbing.

We went over and she was completely angelic, as if a month ago she didn't tell me I was a piece of shit and threaten to ruin the reputation it has taken fifteen years to build. With Glen nearby, I let her feel the baby in my womb, and put her ear to my stomach to hear his little sounds.

It was sort of nice, in a strange, disturbing kind of way. It was sad to notice that I was happier to leave than I was to arrive. I know it sounds crazy, but I kept thinking about Marvin Gaye and how he was killed by his own father.

As a mother-to-be, I feel I have to look at these feelings, no matter how far-fetched they may seem. My protective instinct is way up, and there's no way I am going to ignore it. It is abundantly clear that between my mother and me, I am the only one focusing on what my baby needs.

July 20

Feeling much better today. I woke up with that blissed-out, "I am pregnant woman, hear me roar" vibe. I must really be hitting the second trimester now. I feel the baby so much, his presence like a little glow in my belly. It's way stronger than the quickening of a few weeks ago, that slight, supersubtle whisper of baby consciousness. Instead of the first hello, the first mutual acknowledgment of what exactly is going on here, now it's like a whole conversation between us.

I am having a baby!

For lunch, Glen and I went to the French restaurant around the corner from the apartment. I am really showing now, and people everywhere we go look at me and smile and ask questions. There was a bit of a wait at the restaurant and the couple in front of us gave us their space in line. The woman said she remembered what it was like to be pregnant and hungry in a room full of other people eating.

That is happening more and more, random women starting conversations about the trials and tribulations of pregnancy. I can tell by the way Glen shuts down when they approach that he finds it intrusive and strange, but I like it. It's the first club I've unequivocally belonged to, and I understand tribalism much more as a result. The world really does become divided into the people who know this land and those who don't.

Over lunch Glen and I talked about the amnio, for which I have now missed three appointments. In my opinion, we've already done the pre-amnio blood-test version of the amnio, which came back normal, with no indication of Down's or anything else, so why push it? The amnio would be a follow-up to that, a just-to-make-sure kind of thing, and we'd get to find out boy or girl. Glen says it is up to me. He doesn't believe in a lot of tests, the whole cult of getting everything just because we can, just because it is available. In his opinion, the baby is healthy, and if it's not, we'll deal.

I was into the amnio until I read about the one-in-three-hundred chance of miscarriage. No one I know has ever had a problem, but I just can't get too excited about a huge needle that close to my baby. On the other hand, I have to be honest with myself about being able to care for a baby with special needs. I don't think I can do it. And I definitely want to know ahead of time so that I can make an informed decision. On the third hand, I read that it is not unusual to get a false positive, and then you're really in the wringer.

After we ate, I got really, really tired and came home and went to sleep. I woke up still tired and with that run-down feeling that comes, I think, with a low red blood cell count. Sonam says that even though I am sick, I have to find a way to keep exercising, even if it is just a little. If I feel better tomorrow, I will go for a swim in the morning before I sit down to work.

July 21

Speaking of work. I have no desire to do any. My mind just doesn't have any sparkle, which I find alarming, since my job basically depends on sparkle.

Went to a prenatal appointment at Dr. Lowen's. I mentioned

that after the hospital visit I am thinking even more about a home birth. She said, You know, you have to make sure you've got your priorities straight. It's okay to have a baby at home, but a home birth is more for the mother. You go to the hospital for the baby.

My first reaction was anger: How dare she pit me against my baby! If it's better for me, it will be better for the baby. But then I started thinking about the baby, and how wrecked I would be if something went wrong. I remembered my stepmother saying that if something happened to the baby I would never forgive myself. She's right.

Glen is still against a home birth, and when I showed him *The Birth Book,* which Carl and Martine gave me, with all of the amazing pictures of people looking all natural and groovy and organic and healthy, he said, Yes, but they don't put the pictures of home births gone wrong in the book, you don't see those pictures. To which I countered that they don't tell you about the hospital births gone horribly wrong, either. They don't take pictures of all of the C-sectioned moms that could have had natural births. They don't blow up pictures of episiotomies and put them up on the wall next to the cute one-year-olds.

We did another blood test. Dr. Lowen doesn't have any idea why I had the reaction I did to the antibiotics, and isn't quite sure what to make of the fact that my counts aren't back to normal, but she is reassured that now they are going up, and not down.

Me, too.

July 27

I spent a good hour this morning standing in the kitchen in my underwear trying to figure out new and exciting ways to ingest iron-rich molasses. First I tried heating soymilk and dissolving the molasses in it, kind of like a molasses hot chocolate. Barf. Then I tried spreading it like peanut butter on toast. Super barf. Then I tried just sucking on a spoonful. Oh my God, I almost passed out, it was so disgusting.

Solomon arrives in a couple of days for orientation at the new school we decided to send him to here in Berkeley. His mother found an apartment close to the school, and we have agreed that he should live with her primarily, and see me on weekends, and for meals during the week.

I am nervous about the whole arrangement and feeling over-whelmed. I am not going to be able to take care of him as much as I usually do, but I don't want him to feel displaced by the baby. To calm my nerves I made a little schedule that includes a few things I know he'll like. He's old enough to take care of himself a bit, and also be helpful to me. Right?

August 1

Solomon left today. He didn't help, exactly, but I did enjoy hanging out with him. Even though I am ginormous for five months, I can tell the baby thing is a bit abstract to him. I had to keep reminding him that I can't do the things I used to do, like walk up five flights of stairs. Or work all day, go out for dinner, a movie, and then to the bookstore to look at magazines.

Orientation at his new school seemed to go well. He came back with a big smile on his face and several new "friends." He didn't want to hear the lecture I gave him about throwing the word "friend" around with people you hardly know, though. After a few minutes he was like, Okay! Can we go to the burrito place now?

Last night Glen and I talked about the difference between

mothering and smothering. Mothering has to do with setting appropriate boundaries and giving kids room to be themselves. Smothering has to do with projecting all of your fears and anxieties onto kids and not giving them a moment's peace. I am determined to do the former and not the latter, but it isn't easy. I notice how much I problematize different aspects of Solomon's identity, calling attention to behaviors that aren't just so and constantly making little corrections. I notice that I want to know his thoughts and feelings a little too much.

I asked Glen about his mother, and what she did right in raising him. She was abandoned as an infant, he said, and ended up graduating from Boston University at a time when very few women, and even fewer African-American women, were able to do so. She was also a single mother at a time when it was socially taboo. She went to graduate school, and then worked as a counselor in a women's prison for twenty-six years.

Tears didn't well up in Glen's eyes, but I could tell he was moved remembering her fortitude. She worked long hours, he said, but he always had a hot dinner, and never felt that he had to fend for himself. She created such a strong network of friends that he always felt he had three or four mothers. She gave him room, he continued, but she was also clear about her expectations. "I did well in school," he said, "lettered in three sports, and almost died of mortification whenever I did something she didn't approve."

She wasn't a saint, he said, but she made some choices to ensure that he would have a better life. "The most important thing she did was move us from New York to California, to give me a chance to grow up without the judgment that came with being a child born out of wedlock in a community where everyone gossiped." He paused. "She let go of everything she knew, family, friends, community, to give me an opportunity to live free of that burden, and looking back now, I'm sure it saved my life."

We kept talking about their relationship. Glen left graduate school just before getting his master's degree to care for her when she was ill and then dying of cancer. At one point in the conversation, he said something that he often says when we discuss raising children and the state of masculinity: "Boys need their mothers."

It wasn't the first time we've talked about his mother and the decisions she made, but after the last encounter with my own mother, I can relate a little more to the idea of leaving what is familiar to create a happy life for your child. I can see the importance of making decisions that enable your child to be not just physically safe in an environment, but emotionally and psychologically safe as well. If the well-being of my own child doesn't inspire me to break through my ambivalence about a person or situation and act more decisively, I have no idea what will.

August 2

I've started swimming. Tonight it was just a teenaged couple and me wading around in the fog. A few nights ago it was me and an older woman who swims every day at nine. Both swims were relaxing. I could see the lights of the city through the steam rising off the pool, and the water was soothing and warm. So far, the baby seems to love being in the water. I imagine he goes right to sleep as I stroke and glide.

On Saturday, I made the mistake of going swimming in the middle of the day, when the pool was overrun with, in my humble opinion, bratty, privileged kids. They bumped into me, swam across my lane, threw footballs over my head, and generally ran around paying no attention to anyone but themselves. I kept standing in the shallow end at the break in my laps so that their mothers would see that I was no ordinary lap swimmer, I was a *pregnant* lap swimmer, damn it. I deserved some modicum of respect, even if just for safety. But the mothers ignored me, too, and kept chatting and glancing approvingly at their kids as they whooped all around me.

The whole time I was thinking about how I will be with the baby, and how he will never be so rude and how I as a parent will never be so checked out. Then I thought, Well, maybe those moms are over there talking about their mastectomies or their husbands' affairs. Maybe this is the first break they've had in weeks. Who knows? They could have been talking about their vacation in Tahiti, but I certainly felt less bitchy toward them when I imagined that they, like everyone else, have problems.

August 4

Glen and I went to have the amnio. We went, even though I was on the fence and even though if there were something wrong it would be too late to do anything about it. "Something wrong" being Down syndrome or worse. "Anything about it" being an abortion.

The receptionist warned me that it would be a three-hour appointment, because in addition to the procedure itself, I would need to undergo routine counseling. She didn't say what kind, and when I asked, she made it sound like preparatory counseling, like you might get before taking an HIV test. How to be prepared for the worst. When we got there, the counseling, which we had to agree to have before they would administer the amnio, turned out to really be "genetic counseling." We were taken into a little room by someone who worked not for the hospital but for a biotech company based in Los Angeles. This very nice woman proceeded to do a "genetic intake" on me and Glen, asking about the race, national origin, and health of family members as far back as we could remember.

The flow from signing in to sitting in the woman's office was so seamless that it took me about ten minutes to realize that something other than what I expected was going on. I was, like I suspect most of the young and middle-aged women in the waiting room, so focused on doing something beneficial for my baby and so excited about seeing him in the ultrasound preceding the amnio that the nice woman could have been asking for rights to my firstborn's stem cells and I wouldn't have noticed.

Glen was less distracted, and as I felt his discomfort I asked the relevance of the information being gathered. I also asked who would own the information, and if my privacy was protected by law. Again, call me paranoid, but I saw the movie *Gattaca*. Genetic discrimination, though not as prevalent today as other forms of discrimination, is not just a paranoid delusion. We don't know what kind of world our children will inherit.

The very nice woman explained that this was a way to screen for potential genetic disorders. She explained that all the information was confidential, and that her computer linked only to the company's database and she had to have a special access code to even turn it on. She explained that the results, my baby's genetic tree, would be shipped to a completely secure facility somewhere in Southern California. She explained that there are, in fact, laws in place that prohibit her company or any other company from using the information for testing, research, or anything else.

I started to feel very uncomfortable. How harmless could it be if it required so much security? It is not too difficult to imagine my son's genes being used against him. If he is predisposed to sickle-cell anemia and heart disease, for example, and potential employers can call this up with a stroke of the keyboard, will this make him less employable? If insurers can call up a family history of diabetes, dementia, or some other disease that is costly to maintain, will they insure him? At what price? These are only two scenarios that gave me pause. I shared them with the very nice woman, and she reminded me about the laws. I reminded her that laws change, you know, and usually to facilitate economic expansion. I can't think of another industry with as much momentum as biotech.

I think she was shocked when I decided against the amnio, but she tried to appear nonjudgmental and supportive. I was a little shocked myself. Amnios are as common as breastfeeding. Even though I was on the fence, I never really thought I'd go through my pregnancy without having one. But what can I say? When she told me that she wasn't sure, exactly, where the fluid was transferred after the test, I lost faith in the whole system. Was I sure I could handle a child with special needs? Absolutely not. Did I feel certain that my baby was going to be more than healthy? Absolutely. Was that anything other than magical thinking? Hard to say.

I did go for the ultrasound, though. To make sure the baby has all ten fingers and toes and both legs and arms, and none of the early signs of other problems. There was also the issue of finding out the sex.

As I lay naked from the waist down on the metal table with cold gel slathered across my belly, a woman who has been doing ultrasounds for thirty years zipped from one side of my baby's face to the other, one hand to the other, one organ to the other. After a few clicks and a few anxious questions from me about whether or not everything looked normal, she asked if we wanted to know if our child was a girl or a boy. I looked at Glen and he said it was up to me. I've never been able to stand someone else knowing something I don't, so I said yes. Well, the technician said, he's definitely a boy. Without a doubt.

A boy!

I knew it.

My boy!

Then she showed us his face and butt and elbow, none of which were the least bit identifiable to me.

As my son squirmed in response to her prodding and poking, at one point turning all the way around to avoid her probe, I wondered aloud if we might be disturbing him with all of our measuring. The woman looked at me with, what can I call it? Disdain? Condescension? I shook my head, trying to meet her halfway, after all, she *had* spent thirty years doing this. I'm just a newbie. That's ridiculous, she said. You're just projecting. And then she roughly wiped a fraction of the gunk off my stomach and told me to wait for the doctor.

It is an understatement to say that I was ready to go home after all this. Maybe I am just hormonally challenged, but as we walked into the bright sun of the parking lot I thought about how fiercely protective I am of this being growing inside of me. That medical office might as well have been a lion on the prowl for fresh kill.

I felt a sense of dread as I wondered about the hundreds of skirmishes before me, and the long and obstinate arm of the culture reaching into my boy's mind and possibly into his very DNA. I clutched Glen's arm more tightly, straining to imagine how I would negotiate it all without his stable presence and fierce intelligence.

Together, we might be able to make it. Alone, I am not so sure.

Five

OH, that it were possible to write about having a baby in America without writing about not having a baby. I am talking about abortion of course, arguably one of the most controversial medical procedures of our time. As I write, teenagers are taking up collections to travel across state lines to "terminate," and twenty-something women are giving birth to babies they don't want and can't take care of because they think abortion is murder. Right this second, medical students are protesting the ban on teaching them how to perform abortions, and doctors are being stalked and murdered for making abortions available.

In our country, the issue of abortion is used as a litmus test for personal morality and political loyalty, which makes writing about having one dangerous. It doesn't matter that more than one million women have abortions every year, or that you would be hard-pressed to find a family or group of friends in which no one had gone through the ordeal. The moment you talk about abortion publicly, you run the risk of being attacked. Or your story being co-opted and pressed into service.

A few months ago, I was doing research for an article. Amid the 679,000 entries that flashed across my screen, I came across my name in the blog of someone claiming to be a former classmate. He cited a piece I wrote a decade ago on using an abortion as an opportunity to reflect on what life would be like if women were forced to bear children they didn't want. In an attempt to provide a counterpoint to the emotional trauma of abortion, I posited a way to think about the choice as an empowering option that was the result of many years of political struggle.

But the blogger didn't see the piece in this context, and accused me of being "defiantly proud" of having had an abortion, and of "coming close to suggesting that it would be a good thing if all women had abortions." Both of these statements, in my view, were gross misinterpretations, and yet I supposed they were also understandable extrapolations in light of the author's point of view.

Continuing my search, I began to think about approaching actions in terms of their result rather than their "truth." The question was not whether the blogger's statements were "true"—they were not to me but were very much so to him. The question was about the result of his statements. What is the effect of saying that I am proud of having had an abortion, and that I think it would be a good thing for all women to have one?

I ask because when I think about conceiving a child at thirty-four, carrying and giving birth to another human being, I have to revisit the experience of conceiving and not carrying, conceiving and not giving birth to another human being. I have to revisit this because the two are inextricably linked. I have to preface the discussion because it would be easy to distort what I write here and use the distortion as another log on the out-of-control bonfire that is the abortion debate in America.

That is not my intention.

I had an abortion at fourteen, in a little medical office on Geary Street in San Francisco, in what was then called the French Medical Building. It was a foggy San Francisco day and I was wearing pink *Flashdance*-y leg warmers over the calves of my faded jeans. The procedure itself was uneventful. I remember a hideously long needle and then the pain of it piercing my cervix, followed by the whirring of a machine. I remember the doctor, a severe, quiet, older woman with small hands and gray hair. I remember the assistant telling me what was happening, step by step. I remember it being over much more quickly than I anticipated and feeling relief as I walked out of the building and felt the cool San Francisco air against my face.

For years I thought very little about the experience. It was behind me, a choice I made to save my life, a choice I made because there was no other choice. At the time, I lived with my mother in a small apartment in a modest neighborhood. I had just finished the ninth grade. I was headed to a private school that held much promise. I loved my boyfriend, but I was a child, and so was he. Though my boyfriend would second-guess our decision twenty years later, at the time I did not. I added it to the list of experiences that made me who I was at the time: a young woman who had been through a lot. A young woman who was beginning to expect that life would be difficult, complicated, painful.

It wasn't until college that I began to think about the abortion, to reflect on it as a series of moments—the needle, the doctor, the subsequent blocking out of any emotion connected to the event—that lurked in the crevices of my mind, powerfully shaping my self-image. But in college, political necessities took center stage. I was more invested in fighting for the right of women to have abortions than I was in fighting for my right to wade through the aftermath of having my own.

But there was aftermath, and when I decided I wanted to have a baby, it came flying up at me in the form of a mocking, conspiratorial inner voice. This voice attacked my self-esteem. It challenged the idea that having a baby was something my body could actually do. It said awful things. Things like, The doctor sterilized you, remember? And, Your womb is too damaged now to conceive, let alone carry something as beautiful and important as a baby!

I tried to ignore the voice, to shake it off, but where it had been barely audible before, when I started trying to get pregnant it turned ruthless. In the beginning, I battled it alone, and acknowledged it only when talking to gynecologists. I insisted they convince me I wasn't broken, that having had an abortion did not lower my chance of a successful pregnancy. The doctors looked at me strangely when I pressed them for reassurance. I think it shocked them that I, a "modern woman," would have such fears.

But I did have those fears. Before I became pregnant, they came in the form of the face I sometimes saw in my mind's eye: the Being that hovered. She was a she, with large, dark eyes and an easy laugh. She looked at me, not with anger or blame, but with a quiet sadness. We missed our time, her face said to me. I made it to you but you weren't ready.

I do not regret having the abortion. I regret being lonely and having sex so young, that the Pill was not foolproof, that the permissive culture around me did nothing to prepare me for its consequences. But the abortion itself I do not regret. It is only that I have had to learn to manage the aftermath. First to acknowledge that it exists, and then to reroute it when it appears, to re-lay the cables in my mind so that A no longer connects to E.

Because ultimately, I could not hurl myself into the future and keep a death grip on the past at the same time. I had to wade through the muck, to wake up to the poisonous thoughts I hoarded like jewels. I found that there was a time and a place where I lost faith in my body's ability to sustain new life. There was a time and a place where doubt and shame took the space where hope and confidence should be.

This work of looking, grieving, and reframing didn't take place in a therapist's office, but with Glen, the man I chose to be the father of my child. I told him all of my fears and he held every one, countering what needed to be countered, persevering against all odds to prove me wrong. He told me about abortions he supported women through, and we spoke of the scars that sometimes never heal because the nonpartisan language of healing cannot blossom in a field of polemic.

In these conversations, the mocking voice began to face the inevitability of its defeat. It was silent at first only for a few moments, but then for longer and longer periods until I was pregnant. The miraculous event shattered its credibility forever.

August 7

Talked with Trajal last night until I couldn't talk anymore. He's going to throw me a baby shower. So sweet. We talked about who should host it with him, where it should be, and how I have to get the registry together. I love the idea of lots of people I like and love welcoming my baby into the world.

Our talking marathon reminded me of college. We used to stay up all night talking about race, gender, art, sexuality, and the latest Madonna video. All while writing papers with titles like "Isolation and Redemption in the Novels of Edith Wharton," "Man as Totem in Abstract Expressionism," and "Sign and Signifier in the Hip-Hop Nation."

Now we're weighing the pros and cons of co-sleepers.

Is this what it means to grow up? I feel exactly the same, just focused on different feelings, images, products, and a little more tired.

I went online this morning and started dealing with the registry. Setting one up means I have to pick some stuff, and that means making decisions. I am especially bananas over the stroller question. Should I get the "travel system" with the car seat that pops between the stroller and the car? The Euro bathtub? *The Happiest Baby on the Block* video?

I was online only for a couple of hours, but I am already feeling overwhelmed by the pregnancy industry. Those marketers just reach right in and get us first-time moms because we don't have a clue what we'll really need. I know that I feel so much anxiety about being ill prepared emotionally and psychologically that I'll buy anything and everything to soothe my jangled first-timer nerves.

On that front, I have embarked upon the massage aspect of my pregnancy. I found a great massage therapist who does this out-of-control prenatal thing with pillows and heating pads and sandalwood oil. I just lie there like a beached whale being slathered and rubbed and relieved of aches and pains I didn't even know I had. It was heaven to surrender to the dimly lit room, Japanese flute music, and tiny dendrobiums in porcelain vases. Of course I had to ask him if he had kids. He said, Oh yes, and my wife insisted I massage her like this every day when she was pregnant.

Lucky, lucky, woman.

August 8

Got a call today from the "genetic counselor"! She thinks that perhaps I have G-6-pd deficiency, a genetic blood disorder that makes all sulfa antibiotics practically lethal, along with random foods like fava beans. She said that may be why I had the reaction in the hospital. It may also explain why I got so sick many years ago in Egypt: I was eating fava beans every single day.

Go figure. The woman I thought was Satan may have just given me my genetic key. If she's right, knowing that I have this disorder could save my life.

Also got an interesting request from a magazine to interview Arthur Miller. I said yes, but after thinking about it, I think I'd rather interview Rebecca, his daughter. I remain interested in the children who manage to emerge from the shadow of well-known parentage. So few make it. Then there's the sobering truth that no matter what you go through, it's like being the poor little rich kid: People just think you're whining. No one wants to hear that adults who grew up in a rarefied world have serious issues. They just don't. You're supposed to shut up and take your last name to the bank.

There ought to be a how-to book for parents in the public eye on how to raise sane, happy kids. I hope one day to be able to write it.

August 9

I have started to look at thin women with something akin to envy. I feel so huge, so invisible in my unfashionableness. This morning I caught myself clocking the straight-leg jeans of a woman in front of me, the pointy little shoes, the body-fitting top. I had never noticed how thin these put-together young women are. How thin I guess I used to be, how young and unaffected.

Now I am awkward and wide, puffy where I used to be angular. At my last appointment with Dr. Lowen, I weighed 165 pounds. That's thirty-five pounds gained, and I'm only in the fifth month. When the nurse's eyes widened, I said, Hey, what can I say, he's healthy and robust, remember? He likes to eat.

But it's more than the weight gain, it's the sense of not being able to turn back. I won't ever be as young as that young woman again. I may be that thin, though I can't quite imagine it, but I will never again be that pristine, totally willful young woman. This descent into powerlessness, and being at the whim of a force infinitely stronger than me, has changed me forever.

I always thought I would appreciate not being the object of penetrating stares and appraisals, but somehow I don't exactly. In our culture, sexuality is always the subtext, and it feels strange to be excluded from the conversation.

August 10

Have I documented how much this child inside of me likes salad? Oh my God! I could eat ten huge bowls a day and it wouldn't be enough. He also likes black-cherry soda and huge beef hot dogs with sauerkraut and mustard that give me the most wicked heartburn.

Glen introduced me to Tums last night at one a.m., when I couldn't take it anymore and begged him to make it stop. I thought my esophagus was going to catch fire. Yet another gift from the little one: heartburn. I wake up in the middle of the night burping and gulping for air.

Attractive.

August 13

I have officially entered into the heated immunization debate. My friend Chaya told me today that she believes that kids are "altered" after being vaccinated, and that I should do everything in my power to prevent the baby from getting his shots for at least the first year. She says before that, their immune systems are weakened because they haven't had enough time to develop, and this creates all kinds of problems. Their emotional affect is often dampened, and, according to her, there is even a correlation between the vaccines and ADD.

I intuitively agree that shooting a newborn up with a huge dose of a deadly disease (or five or six) seems a bit demented, and yet there are millions of people who have been immunized and are just fine. Heck, I was immunized. But still, I'd prefer not to give him a shot of any kind at birth and for at least six months to a year after. And I don't really see the need to give him a vaccine for a disease that's been eradicated.

There was just enough of the religious in Chaya's voice to give me pause, however. When she gave me the name of a friend of hers who has researched the subject exhaustively, I put it in my book with all the other cards with people's names that I've been given over the last five months. When I got home I started looking for guidance from what Glen calls my other husband, the Internet.

I was a bit shocked to find this statement from Dr. Jane Orient of the Association of American Physicians and Surgeons:

> Measles, mumps, rubella, hepatitis B, and a whole
> panoply of childhood diseases are a far less serious threat
> than having a fraction (say 10%) of a generation afflicted
> with learning disability and/or uncontrollable aggressive
> behavior because of an impassioned crusade for universal
> vaccination.

On the other hand, Children's Hospital of Philadelphia posted this on its site:

Vaccines are considered the best way to protect your child against diseases that could cause liver damage, liver cancer, suffocation, meningitis, pneumonia, paralysis, lockjaw, seizures, brain damage, deafness, blindness, mental retardation, learning disabilities, birth defects, encephalitis or death.

Vaccines are studied extensively for their safety before being recommended for children and continue to be monitored after recommendation. Because vaccines are given to healthy children, they are held to the highest standards of safety.

Vaccines are considered by some to be a civic duty because they create "herd immunity." This means that when most of the people in a community are immunized, there is less opportunity for a disease to enter the community and make people sick. Because there are members of our society that are too young, too weak, or otherwise unable to receive vaccines for medical reasons, they rely on "herd immunity" to keep them well.

When I talked to Glen about it, we came up with the scenario of our great-great-grandkids' deciding against vaccinating their kids against cancer because they hadn't experienced people dying from the disease, and couldn't imagine that there could be a resurgence.

We talked about the risk of driving cars, flying in airplanes, swimming in the ocean. If there was vaccine developed for HIV or cancer, would we get it, knowing there was a one-in-a-million risk of something going wrong? Probably. We talked about how much we travel. Just a few months before I got pregnant, we flew halfway around the world and passed through six different airports. Even if a disease was eradicated in our country, with so much international exposure, wouldn't it be irresponsible to leave our child vulnerable to contracting it in another country?

But what if our son died at two and a half, after a hepatitis B shot? Or of sudden infant death syndrome the night after being vaccinated? Or developed a learning disability that was later linked to a vaccine?

We talked for hours and at the end of it, I was practically in tears. The magnitude of the decisions, my God, does it ever stop?

August 18

Picked my father up from the airport this afternoon and convinced him to rent a huge SUV to help me bring some things up to the house in Mendocino.

It hit me on the line at Hertz: I am almost thirty-five years old and my father is still helping me move my stuff. I remembered the long drive to New Haven on the first day of college. The car was overflowing with clothes and posters and bedding. At the end of the year, he picked me up from an old, funky house I had moved into, fleeing the dorms. I had thrown everything I owned into black garbage bags that he dutifully slung into the back of the Volvo. I thought of him doing the same for my brother and sister, and how endless it must have seemed to him all those years.

Parenting. Again, I have to wonder, does it ever stop?

He told me that I look good, but tired. He said he wanted to come out to support me because he's been worried and knows how difficult my pregnancy has been. I started to cry. It *has* been hard. My tendency is to think about how much worse other people have it, but the truth is, none of this has been easy.

August 19

A whole gang of us went out tonight to do a reading at Borders from *What Makes a Man*. The essayists who read were funny and moving. I did what I seem to do best these days: beamed and rubbed my big belly.

My father's presence is stirring up old feelings. When I lived in California as a young person, he came to visit only once, when I graduated from high school. I flubbed my valedictorian speech because I was so nervous about my parents being in the same space, breathing the same air. Having him here makes me realize how much I longed for him. We were so close and then suddenly, when my parents moved to opposite ends of the country after their divorce, we were far, and I felt disconnected and lost.

Having him here, playing the father role, feels good and right, archetypally correct. He picked me up today, and we went for a walk around the lake in Tilden Park. On the way home, we stopped at the supermarket for preparatory diapers and baby food. He insisted on paying here, in California, the way he always does there, in New York, which made me smile. I don't know if I can describe it, really. But to see him in the grocery store that I go to every few days, looking at the same checkout people under the same fluorescent lights made me feel more integrated, like my life is finally becoming seamless rather than patched together.

It seems right that the baby is the catalyst for this healing. So far he's been the catalyst for so much that is good in my life. Becoming more patient and less argumentative, learning to be a more accepting partner, even eating more salad!

August 20

I am huge. Just fucking ginormous. Whose body is this, anyway? How big can I actually get? Most days I feel like a sensual Amazon of fertility, but sometimes I am just not up to lugging it all around. Part of it is that my counts are still so low. The anemia is making normal activities downright Herculean. This morning it was all I could do to wash a load of clothes, scramble some eggs, and answer a few e-mails. Then I had to take a nap.

My father picked me up in the afternoon in the big boat of a car that he hates driving, but which I love being driven in. It's my size. We went to see *The Manchurian Candidate,* which was a fascinating look at contemporary masculinity. It was a good example of how mothers often participate in the making of a self-sacrificing, money-and-power-at-all-costs, man-a-tron. They shape the boy into a version of the powerful figure they wish they could be; they shape the boy into a version of the husband they wish they had; they shape the boy into someone who is, in ways barely perceptible to the untrained eye, utterly under their control.

I don't want to be like that.

August 25

My father and I had a long talk today about my determination to be happy. The truth is that I am happier now than I have ever been, and I am amazed by how much that has to do with falling in love with this baby inside of me.

As a child of divorce, it has been hard for me to grasp the concept of a functional family dynamic. What does it look like? How does it make you feel? I'm so used to equating family with conflict and psychological wounding, unbridled jealousy and simmering rage, that I've been unknowingly re-creating it in every major relationship I've had.

The pain of those relationships should have been motivation enough to change, but it has taken the desire for my baby to have a different experience to drive me to make different choices. In my role as fearless protector, I have become more decisive and self-aware, less prone to being yanked about by the needs and wants of others. I'm not sure how it happened, but it seems that in being able to love my child unconditionally, I am more able to love myself unconditionally, which means putting up with a lot less bullshit from others.

It's so cliché and remedial, but I think this pregnancy is teaching me that love is about listening to the people you love, and giving them not what you think they should have, but what they say they need. Love is not about endless negotiation, and recovering from blows landed in the throes of anger, but eliminating those fits completely. Family does not have to be a battleground.

The further along I get in this pregnancy journey, the more I realize that my longing for a child was a longing for an opportunity to try it all again. It was a longing to do family better, to do it right. To create happiness not just for my babies, but for me.

August 27

Back from Mendocino, and my father and I are both exhausted from the drive. Productive visit, though.

Before we left, I showed him all of the little changes and upgrades I've made to the place in preparation for the baby. He was underwhelmed by the two-and-a-half-hour drive, and not convinced I should keep pouring money into a house that my mother could, on a whim, ask me to leave.

He's got a point.

August 29

My father left this morning. I cried walking him to the car and made him promise to come back next year. He said of course, he'd have to come spend time with his grandson. It was hard to see him go, but a relief to have Glen's arms to rest in after he was gone.

Sonam came over in the afternoon. We did our usual Doppler and dipstick dance and then talked about doulas, birth assistants who reportedly ensure shorter labors with less of a chance of a C-section or episiotomy. Since I'm revising my birth plan to include Glen's wishes in the scenario, the doula has emerged as a mutually agreeable possibility. She would massage me during labor, and bring me yummy things, and remind me to turn over or try a new position.

Every time I bring up a postpartum doula, though, someone who can wash clothes and cook food for the first two weeks we're home, Glen shakes his head. We'll be fine, he says. Neither of us wants a stranger so deeply embedded in our intimacy, but I can't imagine how I will feel after I give birth. What if I can't get out of bed, or I am less than functional mentally? Glen pats my hand. You were made for this, he says, look how beautifully you're carrying our baby.

That's easy for him to say, I think. But I do feel better after he says it.

September 2

Today I wandered around San Francisco in the neighborhood where I lived as a teenager. I walked up the hill to St. Mary's Cathedral, down through the housing complex with fountains running through it, and past the concrete bench where I sat my first boyfriend down twenty years ago to tell him I was pregnant. I rubbed my belly and talked to the baby the whole way, showing him where I used to live, and where I used to roller-skate, and where I caught the 38 Geary bus to go to school.

I was amazed by how little has changed. We are so used to thinking that everything revolves around us, that the objects in our world are there because we are, and that without us, they wouldn't exist. I realized today how untrue that is, how thousands passed through the same set of buildings, streets, walkways.

I had the sense of being outside of time. Of watching the world stand still while I moved through it. I was born, I live, and I will die, but the sky goes nowhere.

The thoughts could have been disconcerting, but instead I felt liberated. I felt light walking those hills, watching the memories come up and fade away. I finally understand what people mean when they say that everything changes but everything also stays the same. Life happens where those two meet.

September 8

Glen did a teaching at a dharma center in Marin last night, so we drove across the bridge and took the windy road along the Pacific. The center was beautiful, with an organic farm and lovely Japanese-style buildings. I enjoyed the serenity of the place, and the quiet orderliness of the monastic setting. The food was amazing.

I think I was a shock to some of the monastics, waddling around with my big belly. It amazes me that so many people in America think that in order to be Buddhist you must be a monk or nun. They don't know about laypeople and householders; they don't realize that the dharma can be inflected in just about any lifestyle.

The ride home was long and dark. We listened to Carole King and Al Green, and the baby kicked up a storm and demanded that we stop and get a Mounds bar.

This morning I received an e-mail from my mother. She received the invitation to the baby shower in New York and wants to throw me a tea at her house in Berkeley on my birthday in November. It sounds reasonable, but also not. Even though a part of me wants to believe that it isn't a setup of some kind, the other part is hesitant.

Against my better judgment, I wrote back that it sounds like a great idea, and I am happy she wants to welcome the baby into her community.

Then I got a really bad headache.

September 12

Interviewed the first potential doula today, Ocean. I liked her until she asked why I'm not having the baby at home. I patiently explained that Glen isn't comfortable with it, and we both want the reassurance of being in the hospital in case something goes wrong. She said that I shouldn't let anyone keep me from the birth experience I want, and I had to explain to her that the birth of my child was not only my experience, but Glen's and the baby's, too. In order for me to have the experience I want, they have to be happy, not just me. Considering the hell I gave Glen on this point, I couldn't believe the words coming out of my mouth. But there they were, and they were true.

Then she asked if I am having the baby at the hospital because I am afraid. And I said, Look, hon, no offense, but I've thought about all of this quite a bit. My decisions are hard-won and I have no desire to have them questioned by someone I met ten minutes ago.

Is it me, or the hormones?

Needless to say, she's not the right person. She may have meant well, but you simply cannot be an advocate for someone and at the same time think you know more about their wants and needs than they do. It's impossible.

I took a long shower after she left and then massaged my belly with magic anti–stretch mark potion number 59.

My blood counts are creeping toward normal. Still low, but definitely getting better.

September 14

Today I ran into a tree. I have gotten so clumsy. This belly gets in the way of seeing more than two inches in front of me, and my sense of balance is completely shot. I went to go look at the hospital and parked around the corner from the emergency lot we would use on the big day. I got out of the car and walked around to the meter, and as I was scooping quarters from the bottom of my purse, *bam!* I smacked my head into a thick branch and almost passed out.

The hospital was okay. The neighborhood is a bit sketchy compared to the hospital near the house, which is tucked away and surrounded by trees. This one is on a big city street with a lot of empty storefronts and homeless people wandering around. The patients are mostly Mexican, Ecuadoran, and Samoan, and the nursing staff, from what I could see, is largely Filipino.

I met Sonam in the Labor and Delivery ward, and she showed me the birthing pool and the room where I will labor. It is very large, with hardwood floors and warm, nonfluorescent light. There are two big windows. It wasn't my living room, but it was nicer than most hospital rooms I've seen. It didn't feel institutional. There were no pale green or gray walls, no cold, polished concrete floors.

I was talking to Sonam and the nurses at the nursing station when a woman in one of the rooms started sobbing and screaming, It hurts! It hurts! over and over again. It was the first time I have heard a woman in active labor, and all I could think was: *Drugs!* I want as natural a birth as possible, but I am no masochist. I want that epidural standing by. And that's what I told Sonam in no uncertain terms as I clutched her arm while waiting for the elevator. Make sure we have an epidural close by. When she smiled, I was like, No, Sonam, you don't understand, I am serious.

She said okay.

I said it again as the elevator doors were closing.

Don't forget the epidural!

September 15

I went to see the osteopath today. He's been working on me for years, helping to manage a repetitive strain injury I've had for years that makes writing difficult. He also tends to the aftereffects of a motorcycle accident I had as a teenager, when I thought I could drive a motorcycle around a semi-developed island in a bikini and flip-flops.

He was excited about the baby and told me about all the pregnant women he's treated. When I asked if he had children, he said that he and his first wife had been pregnant, but the baby died at birth from Listeria, a bacterium found in uncooked beef and poultry, and processed foods like hot dogs and deli meats that aren't cooked properly before packaging.

Uch! The heartache. To carry a baby to term and give birth only to have the baby die in the first minutes of life is unbearable to imagine, and yet this happens all over the world, every day. When I told him how sorry I was, he nodded and told me about his second wife and her daughter, with whom he is very close.

My osteopath is such a gentle guy, such a healer. He's so deserving of all kinds of love. He must have been devastated. I stayed cool and kept a good boundary, but really I wanted to get off the table and give him a big hug.

Now that I'm listening, it seems everyone has a birth story, or an almost birth story.

Six

To BE PUT under the heading "What on Earth Was I Thinking?": I first tried to get pregnant while in a passionate relationship with a beautiful, brilliant, and ultimately unfaithful musician. On the road in Tokyo, Århus, Milan, Santa Fe, and other even more exotic climes, the two of us talked about making a baby. Inevitably, the discussion took place in hotel bathrooms—an elegant white marble cube in Bern, a humble ventilated box in North Carolina, a padded art deco creation in Chicago—and on the tour bus, especially after a gig at which a good-looking man had been spotted. A good-looking man who had the requisite physique and the even more requisite over-the-top adoration/obsession for my rock-star girlfriend.

We'd be sprawled on the filthy sofas at the back of the bus at three a.m., still riding the adrenaline from the show and trying not to inhale the exhaust seeping in from the back of the old Prevo.

Undoubtedly she, the girlfriend, would have put a movie into the DVD player, something like *Hair, Dumb and Dumber,* or *Amadeus.* If the band hadn't inhaled it all, we'd be munching on the remains of food listed on her craft-service rider: carrot sticks and hummus, a glass of soymilk. If the band had finished everything, I'd be trying to make a meal out of a bag of cashews scored the previous day at Whole Foods.

During lulls in the action, I would say something like: M would be good. And she would say, Yeah, we should put him on the list. Or, I don't know—he's too goofy. Or, He's not that smart. Or, He's got a great body. Or, He's got a girlfriend who would never, ever let him do it.

We talked in terms of genetic preferences and of men who could be fathers but not intrude on our life. We talked of sperm banks and daddy donors and lifetime parenting partners and new family configurations. When our straight friends had kids, we oohed and aahed and declared ourselves godparents, and when our gay friends had kids, we mined them for details. Would the child be close to the other biological parent? Did the donor want involvement? Did it complicate the "primary" relationship?

It was decided that because I wanted the baby most, and because she had already given birth to one child, I would be the one to conceive. She would be my coach, protector, cook. She would also be responsible for naming the baby because I am awful at naming. And because she was crazy for outrageous biblical names like Hezekiah and Ezekiel, and I didn't have the energy to resist.

Over a couple of years, we amassed quite a list of willing participants, though I am not completely sure why they were willing. Was it the prospect of being a father sans the daily work of parenthood?

The promise of free concert tickets for life? Whatever the reason, when all was said and done, it came down to two men who weren't on our list, two men we knew and loved, two men who were already like family. And so, acting as if our relationship was far more stable and full of fidelity than it actually—I found out later— was, my girlfriend and I masked our nervousness with jocular banter and popped the question.

The proposal went something like this: How would you like to have a baby with us? We've thought about it, and, well, you're one of the only people in the world we can imagine doing this with. Sure, we'd like you to be involved because children need fathers, but you could choose your involvement level. Oh, and we want to get pregnant the natural way, no turkey basters. Is that all right with you?

When we initially proposed, the man I favored immediately took himself out of the running. He had been privy to too many of our conversations in which we reduced men to their genetic attributes. He declared that our relationship was intimate enough, thank you very much. Besides, he said with a Cheshire grin, he didn't know where things might go if we started having sex. I laughed when he said this, and stole a look at strong, beautiful hands. I didn't disagree.

Our second choice was a man who had been close to my girl-friend for many years in several capacities. John was loyal, kind, and intelligent. He picked us up from the airport. He counseled the girlfriend through each of her several dozen career crises. He had already taken on the responsibility of fathering two children who were not his own, and one of them had just been accepted to Harvard. John was also an athlete, an attribute I found particularly alluring. By the time we proposed, he had come to rest in the position of brother, or, at the very least, lifelong friend.

I liked John.

We asked John in a more gradual way, over time, using the same questions and phrases, but spaced over months and interlaced with conversations about travel, business, and politics. We asked him to father our child in the way his thoughtful and methodical personality demanded: with gravity, sensitivity, and as much tact as we could muster. Because he was already so embedded in our lives, the proposition was not as much about having a baby as it was about extending our life together and building a nontraditional but committed family.

We talked seriously about moving to Europe, where the girlfriend had a big following, and where I could write and be cared for by the thriving holistic midwifery and healing network. I could learn French, and the baby could be bilingual, and we could live in one of those charming villages in Switzerland in the crook of a mountain road overlooking Lake Geneva, a few miles from the Evian spring. Or we could move to South Africa, where the girlfriend had a big following, and where we could be surrounded by black people deep in the inspirational throes of the project of self-determination. John could be our business manager. John could be our husband.

John was not opposed to the idea, or should I say the fantasy, but this is where it began to get messy. In addition to having dreams of his own of living in Cuba, he was not altogether sure that he wanted to enter our relationship. For one thing, the girlfriend and I fought a lot, and for another thing, John had his own idealistic visions of family, and these visions did not necessarily include two additional women, no matter how dynamic.

There was also the not-minor hindrance of his girlfriend, a woman he'd known since high school and had been involved with for several months. During our discussions, we were surprised to find out that John liked this woman a great deal, that is, when he wasn't talking to us about not liking her and not knowing how to get out of the relationship.

And so it was in the very familiar soup of ambivalence and ambiguity that we began our crazy, rather irresponsible, and beautiful science experiment of trying to make a baby with John. The project included serious and somber conversations at restaurants on the Upper West Side of Manhattan, restaurants that were organic, intercultural, and macrobiotic, restaurants that were futuristic stabs at the kind of hybridity we were, ourselves, considering. Seated around tables with chopsticks and carrot juice and brown rice and Chino-Cuban arroz con pollo, we said, Yes, we want to do this; yes, we think this could be a good thing; yes, why not? We love each other, we are already family, right?

Which led to an evening at one of the hotels we liked, a hotel that felt like home not just because the staff gave us a good rate (fans of the girlfriend), but because we had lived there one summer in a beautiful beige-and-white room that overlooked Broadway and the gorgeous old apartment buildings that line it. I don't remember much of the encounter, only that I concentrated very hard on getting pregnant. And that the next morning I crawled out from under John's heavy limbs and made my way to the bathroom. Steadying myself amid the brushed aluminum and stylized black-and-white prints of orchids, I looked at myself in the mirror and wondered: Is this the face of a pregnant woman? Then I stumbled into an armchair and scribbled a few lines in my journal.

Since accompanying my girlfriend on the road, I used my journal to keep track of our comings and goings. On the inside covers of dime-store notebooks, I made long lists of cities and dates, and pressed my marked-up backstage passes onto the blank sheets in between. I felt that unless I did this, recorded places and times and some tiny sliver, even if only a sentence, there would be no record of the life streaming through each day. And because I am fundamentally a woman who wants stability, I wanted—no, needed—a record, a way to evoke forever the musicians and fans, the airplane flights and bus trips, the hotel rooms and especially the freak encounters that make life on the road, for all of its drudgery, magical.

(An evening in the aforementioned Swiss village, in an alpine chalet overlooking Lake Geneva, comes to mind. Claude, the legend behind the Montreux Jazz Festival, pulling tapes from his archives and there, in his screening room, Aretha Franklin, twenty years ago, playing the piano and singing her heart out.)

Because these elements were such an integral part of our life, they *were* our life, and because I could not imagine that my girlfriend and I would no longer have this life together, I was forced to think pragmatically about bringing the baby on the road. I had moved around a lot as a child and could romanticize the time on the bus as a nomadic lifestyle full of change and diversity. But did I want my child to have rootlessness as an organizing principle? The girlfriend deemed it possible, but I had major doubts, and my scrawled notes from that morning reflected those doubts. After the date and the city and the evening's activity, I scrawled, Baby on the bus? Nursing on the back of a stinky Prevo?

I cannot swear that the way I remember the rest of this story is exactly the way it played out, but I guarantee that only small details may be inaccurate and not the gist of the thing, not the core event.

There were days of thinking I might be pregnant. Days of waiting and nights of lying in bed trying to figure out how I was going to explain the how of this baby to my extended family and even, to the extent that it was interested, to the world at large.

At the onset of these days—I would say on day two or three—came the news that John and his girlfriend were no longer seeing each other. Around day seven came the news that John was seeing his girlfriend again, but only to process the breakup and/or talk about the possibility of being together in the future. On day fourteen or fifteen, John came to us and told us that the girlfriend, whom he was now not seeing, was pregnant, and even though he wasn't sure he wanted the baby, he wasn't sure he could stop her from having it.

My girlfriend and I were horrified. Outraged. Deeply hurt. There were long, cross-country arguments on cell phones, and immature, hyperbolic disavowals in doorways. I, for one, was never so happy and relieved to get my period, an event that, from my perspective, took everything down a notch, or ten. Months passed. I stopped feeling like I had lost a popularity contest. I stopped feeling like I had lost a fertility contest. Though my girlfriend was devastated and vowed it would never be the same, the family slowly reconvened. We decided to befriend the actual mom-to-be, and even though I am pretty sure we both secretly fantasized she was carrying a baby that would ultimately belong to us, we came to terms with what in private we labeled John's gullibility.

Which is how I came to be holding John's baby and not my own at a restaurant in TriBeCa ten months later. The birth had been traumatic, and this was one of the first days out of the house for mother and son. We were doing a group dinner, the kind the girlfriend and I did a lot as a way of keeping the extended tribe together. We invited John and his girlfriend/not girlfriend and their baby as a way of saying we still love you, there is room in the fold even though you lied to us, or didn't, and even though you chose someone else over us, or didn't.

It was an extraordinary experience—heartbreaking, really—to be eating fish with one hand, and holding in the other a tiny, beautiful creature who should have been mine, could have been mine, but wasn't.

I will never forget it.

September 18

We've arrived in Miami for the Dalai Lama's teaching: World Peace Through Inner Peace. Glen's teacher sponsored the teaching, and we are here as special invited guests, which means attending various gatherings with His Holiness and various dignitaries from all over the world. The first teaching is tomorrow at eight a.m. Khenpo expects close to twenty thousand people to attend, which is amazing because the television is full of hurricane warnings and evacuation notices. Two days ago there was talk of evacuating Miami, but Khenpo held firm. When we asked why he didn't leave, he said that only the people who are afraid of dying are leaving. And then he laughed his huge laugh. When we landed, the sky was blue, not a cloud in sight.

We checked into our hotel last night and I've been luxuriating ever since. They say the architecture is "Mediterranean Revival," but it's more Moorish Italianate to me. Whatever you call it, it's just stunning, with elaborate tile work and impossibly high ceilings. I just came from a nighttime swim in possibly the most amazing pool ever. It's billed as the biggest in the continental United States, and at 700,000 gallons, I believe it. I swam by moonlight with soft jazz playing and palm trees blowing in the breeze. The hotel was built in the twenties and I literally felt I was in a different era, and the flappers were going to come out and put on a show.

As I swam, I imagined that the water was precious purifying nectar, cleansing my mind and body of thoughts of anger, jealousy, and greed. I thought about how there is no new water, and that all of the water on the planet has been here, cycling through its various incarnations, for millions of years. I thought about how that same ancient water is inside of me, and so part of me has also been here for millions of years.

After a while, I flipped onto my back and looked out into the vast night sky. Floating, I wondered about the baby. Where did he come from? How did he get here? Where will he go?

How is it possible that I love him so much?

September 19

Today was the luncheon with His Holiness. He entered the room with his entourage of attendants and bodyguards, bowing and making eye contact with as many people as possible. The electricity in the room was palpable, like it must have been when Kennedy walked into a room, or Gandhi. When he reached the podium, he paused, looked out at everyone, and said that human beings have different hair and different eye color, we wear different clothes and come from different places. But really, he said, at the fundamental level, we are all the same.

I can't do justice to the moment, but it was amazing, an empowerment. For a brief second, and forever after for some, you could actually feel the truth of what he was saying. It wasn't just a social or political idea, but an actual experience of sameness and, ultimately, of a world not chopped up by dualistic thinking.

It was like the sky opened up.

September 20

Tonight after the teachings, we had dinner in the hotel restaurant. A harried mom with baby in tow spotted my huge, unmistakably pregnant belly, and proceeded to tell me her whole story: the difficult pregnancy, the complicated birth, the intense sleep-deprivation. I smiled through the whole litany and then asked her, But is it worth it? And she looked at me like I was crazy. Oh, of course. It's so totally worth it. You won't believe it. It's like no love you've ever known.

I rest my case.

After my late-night swim, I came back to the room and admired myself in the mirror. I am really getting into my pregnant body. I've finally got the full breasts I've always wanted, and my thighs, which I've always considered just a tad larger than ideal, are now in perfect proportion.

As I was standing there, thinking how downright voluptuous I am, Glen came up behind me and shared a sentiment that won him the Best Thing Your Partner Can Say When You Are Pregnant Award. He said, You've never been more beautiful. Which turned me right then and there into a goddess. I felt so powerful, having just bathed in the moonlight, and rubbed some kind of outrageous-smelling Tahitian oil all over my belly, that I had to turn around and give him the biggest, juiciest kiss ever.

September 21

Landed at JFK and was practically blinded by the newspaper headlines: "Yes She Is!" and "Pregnant and Still Thin." Apparently, a TV star presumed heterosexual is in love with a woman, and most of the rich, pregnant women in New York are starving themselves so that they can stay CWP—cute while pregnant. Both headlines had me at hello. I had to stop at Hudson News.

The pregnancy article is horrifying. It seems that women don't want to wear maternity clothes or lose their waistlines, so they restrict their diets and try to subsist on a bottle of water and an apple a day. I guess they're not having the renaissance of self-love brought on by baby love I'm having. Yikes. The whole idea of DWP, dieting while pregnant, makes me sad and *hungry*.

September 23

Last night I told everybody I am thinking about naming the baby Tenzin. My stepmother looked up from her plate and said, Tenzin? What kind of name is that? Then my father said that no matter what I named him, he was going to exercise his right as a grandfather to call him whatever he wanted, which was Chaim. I told them that Tenzin is the Dalai Lama's name and that I can't think of anyone better to be named after. To which my stepmother responded, Isn't there anyone in the family you could name him after? And my father said, Yeah Rebec, what about Samuel? David? Moishe?

I felt like Judas.

Before we arrived at the question of what to name the first biological grandchild of the Leventhal clan, we focused our collective energy on whether or not my sister, an aspiring actress, should take a role on a reality show. My brother and I were vehemently opposed and got so outrageously vocal about the whole thing, with my father chiming in from the sidelines with a "legal perspective" and my step-mother picking at her miso cod and trying not to get involved, that my sister finally had no choice but to accuse us of trying to control her life. She stormed out of the room as I yelled, We are only telling you this because we love you, to which everyone nodded approvingly and my father said, That's right, Rebec, after which my sister slammed her bedroom door.

It was my first dinner with them as a ravenous, two-headed, big-bellied omnivore. My father got a huge kick out of watching me eat two California rolls, one filet mignon yakitori, a giant salad, an order of Agadashi tofu, two bowls of miso soup, and an entire order of steamed vegetable dumplings. He kept beaming and say-ing things like, So you're eating for two, my Rebecca? Eat plenty for my grandson in there, the little schmutzky, and asking if I wanted the rest of his chicken-and-vegetable dish.

September 25

We went to my stepmother's best friend Ronnie's house to break the fast for the Jewish holiday of atonement, Yom Kippur. Jason, Ronnie's black, white, and Jewish son, with whom I used to watch *The Love Boat* and *Fantasy Island* sprawled on his mom's bed, was there with his new girlfriend. She's Cuban, but has never been to Cuba. Of course this possibility didn't occur to me until after I had talked about how beautiful the island is and how the people are so incredible. The blank look on her face tipped me off. Then I started obsessing about how her family must have lost everything in the revolution and they probably hate Fidel or at least have serious and legitimate gripes. Then here I come, a spoiled American, talking about it like just another place I visited and added to my places-I-have-gone-and-now-have-an-opinion-about list. Gross.

The question of naming came up again. Ronnie said, Tenzin? No, I don't like that so much. Then my stepmother said, What are the kids at school going to call him? and my brother said, Ten. My father threw his hands up and said, I like Chaim, and I said, Dad, we talked about this, which we had, earlier in the day. I told him that I would not have anyone, including his grandfather, subjecting my child to even the merest hint of identity confusion. I said, What if Grandma had insisted on calling me Susan? And he paused and said, You're right, I would have told her that your name was Rebecca. But how is he going to get a job with a name like Tenzin?

You know, he said seriously, there is a group of women with names like Shanequa speaking publicly about how their names have kept them from succeeding in the workplace. They're all changing their names to Mary.

I told him that Tenzin was a perfectly respectable name, and part of a tradition at least twenty-five hundred years old.

Then I asked him how many jobs he thought Chaim would get, and we both burst into laughter.

September 26

The shower was yesterday. It blew me away. There were people from so many different parts of my life in one room, and for the first time I felt elation rather than dread at the thought of them all coming together. My East Coast family, the Yale mafia, the literary troupe, some Bay Area peeps who happened to be in the city, the buddies I got to keep after the big breakup, two rugged and beautiful idealists from the days I was running around raising money for nonprofits.

Even though I don't see many of them often, the people who came are definitely a part of my tribe, that ever-expanding crew held together by the resonance of a three-hour talk one night at a club about a relationship, or a series of conversations about a TV show we developed together, or a lunch about an essay that led to a discussion about marriage and kids and where the hell our lives were going. I've never felt happier to be surrounded by such a warm and loving bunch, or more certain I was in the exact right place at the right time.

And yet I kept thinking about the Langston Hughes line: What happens to a dream deferred? Does it dry up, like a raisin in the sun? What happens to all of these memories that dwell in the recesses of the mind like ghosts wandering the halls of some abandoned ruin? Where do these memories go, and what, if anything, do they ultimately mean? At the time, each of the encounters felt so meaningful, as if they were shaping the rest of my life, and yet they have all fallen away as mysteriously as they arose.

I can't help thinking of the shower that way, too. There was the idea of what we were doing, welcoming the baby and showering support and encouragement on the mom-to-be, and that is what we did. But the way we think of it, as a gathering that necessitates and facilitates the next gathering, and on and on until you've built a life, I didn't really feel that. It was more like the whole party was in a bubble flying over Manhattan, and when it was over, the bubble burst and then it was gone.

It reminded me of how I felt when I saw the vulture on the first day I found out I was pregnant. I feel as if the self I knew is fading away, and I have no idea who is coming to take her place.

September 29

Just back from a speaking engagement at Carnegie Mellon. Someone asked if I am experiencing pregnancy as the ultimate in Womanhood. It was an interesting question. I said that I feel more in touch with the animal qualities of the species, rather than the gendered ones. My sense of smell is heightened, I am ferociously protective of my developing offspring, my body is going through changes beyond my control in the service of species survival.

I told her that I really feel like an animal when I am hungry. In those moments, when I am on the hunt for my next meal, I feel out of control, led entirely by instinct. When I get to the food, I can barely observe basic etiquette. I want to tear at the meal, to wolf it down. And it's not all eco-friendly, either. I want big, thick, juicy steaks, and whole chickens. I want four scrambled eggs and six pieces of bacon. And then when I finish all that, I want a box of chocolate-covered donuts.

It's in the fact that instinct takes over, and the body is following intelligence all its own, that I find an inkling of an almost supernatural strength. I've always thought of myself as a pacifist. I painstakingly scoop up beetles and walk them outside. I tenderly coax house-trapped hummingbirds into my hand so that I can set them free without harm. But something else is activated in me now. I could kill someone standing in the way of my baby's fruition. It wouldn't even be that hard. The power to defend is that primal.

The women in the audience looked a little shocked, so I softened it a bit by talking about the other side. The way the pregnancy puts you smack in the middle of the huge mystery of life. The way you can't avoid the not-knowing, no matter how much the intellect tries to get a grip on the situation by taking tests and reading books.

The way all you can do, really, is follow the cues you're getting from inside.

Ravenous, vulnerable, victorious. There is power in all of it.

I told her what I now tell lots of young women who look at me with the huge question mark on their face that I used to have: Being pregnant is the best. I highly recommend it.

I really do.

While your baby may soon slow up growing in length (he measures about 15.7 inches from crown to toe by now), he will continue to gain weight until he's born. . . . His lungs and digestive tract are nearly mature and he's probably been able to open and shut his eyes for a while now, so he can see inside you.

October 5

Talked for a long time last night with Glen. Seemingly out of nowhere I suggested we name the baby Jonah, or maybe David. He went through the roof. Um, hello? We're Buddhist, and more important than that, we made a decision. Please don't tell me your name ambivalence is stirred up.

But it's not ambivalence, it's guilt. I feel like I am letting down the clan. If the baby has a name that doesn't resonate with my family's biblical template, they may not bond with him. He's going to need grandparents. Isn't it my responsibility as a mother to make sure the seeds for these relationships are planted?

I also want him to relate to his roots, to know what it means to be a part of this crazy tribe of people who mix love and arguing like chocolate syrup and milk, who use Yiddish proverbs as terms of endearment, and who manage to find fabulous YSL sandals in the mountain of lame shoes at the Barneys warehouse sale.

Maybe guilt is the mechanism that holds families together. I heard somewhere that human beings, in terms of the way we organize ourselves, most resemble pack animals. As in wolves, dogs, wildebeest. We want everyone in our pack to smell the same. If they don't, we're not sure they're really one of us, and if they're not one of us, how can we trust them?

Biblical name=Smelling the same
Smelling the same=Trust
Trust=Survival
Biblical name=Survival

Sigh.

October 9

Sasha the birthing teacher came over today to teach us about labor. She had lots of props: videos of women squatting their babies out in Brazil, a miniature pelvis complete with slide-through baby doll, a diagram of the ten most helpful positions a labor partner can assume during a birth.

We learned about effacement and dilation and the three stages of labor. We learned about breech births, posterior births, C-sections, and episiotomies. She had me hold a piece of ice in my hand to see how I managed the pain of ice burn. She encouraged me to talk about my fears, and to write down my hopes for the birth.

Two and half hours into the four-hour class, Glen asked the quintessential question: "Where's the penis?" He said that everything thus far was about the vagina and the womb. Since the man was so involved in making the baby, there had to be an equally important role for him in the birth.

As Sarah sputtered about daddies being support people and being emotionally connected throughout the labor, I cracked up and looked at Glen with pride. It was such a classic Glen question, I just had to marvel at him.

We ended up having a long discussion of both the medical and natural childbirth models and the role they each have assigned to men. The medical model puts male doctors and a "masculine" institution in control, and the natural childbirth model relegates men to a relatively passive "support and behold" position.

Glen was interested in neither, and insisted there must be another option, something in between.

He mentioned the video of women squatting in Brazil, and asked Sarah if she had done any research in other cultures about the role of men in childbirth. I mentioned a tribe I read about in which men attach prosthetic babies to their stomachs while their partners are pregnant. During childbirth they beat themselves with dried leaves and branches to share the pain.

Glen raised his eyebrows. He wasn't sure about that, but he liked the idea of looking more deeply into it. I made a mental note to add it to my already bulging list of potential article ideas.

All in all, the class was a good use of our time. By the time Sasha left, I was practically begging her to join my labor team. She's worked as a midwife all over the world and has assisted many, many births. She was smart and had excellent boundaries, which

I always appreciate. But alas, she's traveling with her family in December, and can't make it.

But by then we may have discovered where the penis is in this whole process and won't need her!

October 12

Today a checker at the supermarket told me she is never having a baby. Because I am such a sucker for these random pregnancy conversations, I took the bait and asked why not. She can't stand the idea of dependency, she said. She never wants another human being to need her that much. The whole idea of it makes her sick. I asked her age. Twenty-three. I paused, considering my new role of crusader against maternal ambivalence everywhere. I tried to modulate my voice so I didn't sound like too much of a zealot, and told her she had plenty of time to change her mind. She looked at me as if I'd suggested that she cut off her right arm.

October 18

I met another doula today. She was warm and knowledgeable. She has been a doula for twenty years and is known as the best postpartum doula in the area because of the meals she cooks specifically to fortify breastfeeding moms. I liked her, but I am still not sure about opening up the intimacy of our family to a stranger. The more I think about another human being in our space, the more it feels, I don't know, awkward at best, intrusive at worst.

I told Dr. Lowen yesterday that I have officially decided to switch over to midwifery care for my delivery. She was sad to see me go and reminded me that she usually "lets" the mom have the second baby with a midwife, after they see how she does with the first.

I left her office feeling guilty. Am I making a selfish decision that isn't best for the baby? Why are there so many goddamn decisions to make? And why do they all have such intense consequences? Is motherhood just another word for guilt?

Otherwise, the checkup was normal except that I am humongous. I've gained forty pounds so far and the nurse says I haven't even hit the heavy months yet. She said I am lucky because I'm carrying entirely on my stomach and not in my hips and butt.

Got home and puttered about. I cleaned out the refrigerator and all of the kitchen cabinets, and then moved on to reorganizing the hall closet. Spent an hour looking at beds online. Having a baby means that, in addition to a few other pieces of grown-up furniture, I must acquire a proper bed. It must have a headboard to lean against when nursing. It must be beautiful. It must have some kind of unseen storage element for baby blankets and baby clothes and all the rest of the baby stuff I am accumulating.

It must be sexy.

October 19

Tonight I drove myself to the drugstore for a nail clipper and another bottle of Tums.

Going out alone was eerie. I felt exposed in a way I've never experienced. Being a New Yorker, I am used to walking around at night. I know how to scan for danger without thinking about it. But I've never felt like I should be at home, behind closed doors, because the streets are unsafe. I definitely have never felt that I need to have a man by my side to protect me.

But that is exactly how I felt. It was brutal. I felt like my stomach made me a walking target, as if predators could smell my vulnerability. I had thoughts about being mugged, raped, or kicked in the stomach repeatedly. What an awful, awful way to hurt someone. When I think of all of the women and babies who have endured that kind of violence, my mind goes into spasm. I want to vomit.

Talked with Glen about it when I got home. He of course told me that I should not be driving around at night, alone, six and a half months pregnant. I was infuriated. I should be able to drive around any time I want and not have to worry about being bludgeoned to death. He agreed. You *should* be able to, he said, and hopefully one day you will. The real question is what are you going to do in the meantime?

Indeed.

October 22

Maybe it's that the rain hasn't stopped for three days, but today I am bored out of my mind. I am finally doing what everyone says I should have been doing for the last couple of months, resting, but it feels more like jail.

I have officially moved into the waiting phase of this pregnancy. Because even though I can go out and a part of me wants to go out, I really don't have the energy to go out. I would have to get showered and dressed, climb into the car, start it up, and will it down the freeway. No matter where I decide to go, I would have to acquiesce to being the center of attention. I'd have to pretend I was wearing a shirt with a big arrow pointing to my belly and "Ask me about my baby" emblazoned above it.

I am a lady-in-waiting. I am waiting for the big day, the big event, the arrival of the mystery. I know this is a sacred, spiritual time. I am reveling in the predawn of maternity. I am bonding with my baby. I am storing up energy for the upcoming marathon. I am taking care of myself by not exposing myself or the baby to violence, confusion, and chaos.

I know all of this, and I am grateful that I have the luxury to hole up and hide out. I don't have to do makeovers at the Macy's cosmetics counter, I don't have to harvest rice from sunrise to sunset, I don't have to sit in front of the computer fielding interoffice e-mails because I am worried that while I am on maternity leave someone will steal my job.

I know all of this, but still . . . All I can think about, besides being bored to death, is food. What can I eat next? In the last two hours I have had two bowls of chicken soup, three pieces of toast with chicken, two soy ice cream sandwiches, two huge glasses of organic lemonade, an apple, a pomegranate, and as I write this, I've got designs on a steak, a few pieces of sliced turkey, some brown rice, and an orange. Eat and wait. Eat and wait. Eat and wait. And watch movies. And answer e-mail. And write thank-you notes to the people who gave me gifts at my shower. And rub an infinite variety of oils on my bursting stomach to prevent stretch marks.

Glen says I am peripatetic and that he always knew this would be hard for me. "This" being the slowing down of my mind and body, the near cessation of my endless roam. I shake my head at him and think to myself that I understand that this is necessary for family life. I know I don't want to re-create my hypermobile childhood for this little baby.

But there is a secret part of me that thinks he might be right. Who are you kidding? the little voice says. You have a nomadic heart, do you not? You have learned that wherever you go that's where you are, but gosh, you sure like getting there and meeting yourself again.

Seven

TWO VERY POWERFUL and influential women were on television a few weeks ago, speaking triumphantly about the fact that they don't need men. I understand that. If you can financially provide for yourself, you are no longer dependent on another for economic support. I get it. But there are so many other kinds of support. When I think about trying to have this baby alone, without an intimate other to console me when I am worried and cook for me when I am so nauseated I can barely look at the kitchen, let alone stand in it, my head starts spinning. I understand the wisdom of having good friends to get these needs met, but really, I think we need partners in life.

I don't know if it's because I am a child of divorce, a Gen Xer accustomed to relating primarily though e-mail, or the daughter of a women's movement ambivalent about the institution of marriage, but until I met Glen, partnership was elusive. My relationships, while not lacking in intensity, lacked the magical togetherness quotient you find in healthily fused adults. I had never achieved the ineffable calm of couples that don't finish each other's sentences, not because they can't, but because they'd rather be quietly support-ive of each other instead. I had never been half of a couple that checked in several times a day, no matter how mundane the con-versation, to calibrate their movement as a unit from afar.

The most significant obstacle I faced to joining the club of the deeply, truly committed was my complete and utter ignorance of the importance of partner choice. I simply did not understand the necessity of intellectual compatibility and, even more important, *emotional reciprocity* in relationship. I now believe that there should come a time in every young woman's life when a more experienced loved one explains this absolute key point. It's not about marrying for love or money, it's about partnering for sanity, survivability, and the calculable probability that together the two of you will create something more gorgeous and powerful than you ever could alone.

As I've already described, there was also my religion to contend with: absolute autonomy. I would rather die than give up travel, sex-ual freedom, financial independence, and the cordoned-off secret section of my psyche where only I could roam. I kid you not: When I met Glen, I thought I could have a baby with him and another with Ade in Africa, shuttling back and forth every six months. It wasn't until Glen reminded me that I almost died in Africa, and then gently suggested that my plan was completely unrealistic *in terms of main-taining intimacy,* that I realized I needed to get real and throw down the anchor.

I didn't have a visceral sense of what it might be like to merge with something or someone other than myself until I was thirty years old and listening to the Dalai Lama. He was talking about the myth of independence. If you are so independent, he asked, who grows your food? Who sews your clothes, builds your house, makes sure that water comes out of your showerhead? How were you even born? The fact is, he said, we have not done one single thing alone, without the help of a small army of others, and yet we walk around talking about the necessity and supremacy of independence. It's completely irrational.

For a brief moment I felt a softening of my self-perception, a relaxation of my ideas about where I stopped and other people began, a letting go into inseparability. I was not autonomous and never would be. What a relief! The Dalai Lama went on to say that no condition we find ourselves in is permanent. Rich people can become poor. Healthy people can become sick. Young people become old.

I flashed on this while watching the two women on television: the powerful and self-sufficient will become not so powerful and not so self-sufficient. These dynamic women for whom I have a tremendous amount of respect will both need someone at some point. I would wager that it would be more satisfying to them both if this someone did not have to be paid to show up.

I am not blaming feminism, because without parity and equality, partnership is just another word for exploitation. But I am suggesting we take another look at what we're thinking and saying in the name of "empowerment," and how that shapes our actual lives and impacts the people we love. As a mother, I worry about how it makes boys and men feel to hear they are not needed, and can be made obsolete by the presence of enough money and a few good girlfriends. I worry about how it makes them feel to hear that we don't care if they disappear from the face of the earth because we have enough frozen sperm to get us through the foreseeable future. And what about the millions of women who can't afford to not need men? Is empowerment impossible for them?

The more I learn about partnership, the more certain I am that the male partners of the women on television already put up with a tremendous amount of stress and strain just being the husbands of two very powerful, very visible women. Do you think they want to be more or less present, more or less intimate with their wives, after hearing that they aren't really necessary? I know how I would feel if the person I devoted my life to told millions of people he didn't need me.

Wrecked.

Because the fact is that we do need each other, and we are locked into this dance with the whole frickin' world whether we like it or not. This lack of separateness is awful and terrifying, amazing and exhilarating, and just plain true. It seems to me that men and women both need to come up to speed on this, instead of competing for the prize of who can do without whom for longer. There is power in partnership, otherwise the modern, government-sanctioned version of it, marriage, wouldn't be able to hold.

But I began this mini-manifesto simply because I have never felt as much dependence on another person, male or female, as I do now that I am pregnant. Granted, I do feel a tremendous power, a sort of Yes, I've got the fetus now, no one can stop me, but then when that necessarily subsides and I think about the thousands of decisions that are going to come up, the millions of moments where it will inevitably take two heads screwed on right to muddle through, I feel a tremendous need. To be a single mother, while I feel I could do it, at the moment seems a Herculean task.

What I need is a partner: someone who will show up. And what I need to become is a partner: someone who will open the door. I have no idea if I can sustain it as long as I want, which is forever, but I've never felt so motivated to try.

October 24

Blessed be the editors, for they giveth work!

I spoke today with the editor of a high school English textbook I am writing an essay and teaching section for, and he put me on task. I have several subsections to write, answering questions like: What is the difference between an article and an essay? and What is my writing process like?

I decided to write the main essay for the textbook on hip-hop culture and what it was like before it became a global commodity. It's a personal piece about living in the Bronx in the eighties when it all began. And how, as a youth movement, hip-hop was about kids being free and expressive and having a good time. Most important, it was about kids from different cultures finding a common language.

Anyway. It's not like I don't have a whole other book to write, but it is nice to have a few short pieces to focus on. Otherwise, I watch way too much TV. It's just so nice to lie about, clicking the remote. Right now I am in love with *Girlfriends* and *The King of Queens*. I'm convinced these shows are helping me bridge the chasm between single urban professional and suburban nuclear. My life at the moment is two parts *Girlfriends,* two parts *The King of Queens,* one part Discovery Channel.

Good news: I read on the Internet that mothers who eat a lot of chocolate when they are pregnant have happier babies.

November 4

The baby is super-awake today. I sense his awareness more than ever, that he's waking up and taking things in. I've started talking to him, out loud instead of just in my head. I tell him all of the things we're doing, like getting the car washed and driving to the chiropractor, buying laundry detergent and calling Grandpa on the phone. This morning I told him about Sonam and that she's going to be with us in the hospital. I told him not to be afraid because she has delivered hundreds of babies and she loves us.

It's all so exciting, but between interviewing doulas, training for the labor marathon, making sure I've got the right breast pump, and eating everything in sight, I'm totally exhausted. I get why people have their babies in the hospital. It's the planning, stupid! I feel like I'm making a Hollywood film with a two-person crew. If I were to have this baby at home, I would have to do all of what I am already doing, plus shop for plastic sheets and a fifty-foot hose for the water tank.

I'm finally convinced I've made the right decision. I just want to go to the hospital, have this baby, and then come home to a sane, stable environment. I know it sounds rough, but I have a hunch that giving birth is going to be hard enough. I don't also have to transform my apartment into a frickin' birthing center.

November 7

Since I haven't heard from my mother about the birthday tea since she brought it up two months ago, and since I've been feeling a bit sketchy about the whole thing anyway, I wrote her a note telling her that I don't feel comfortable moving forward with what I could only imagine wasn't really going to happen anyway, seeing as how my birthday is in ten days. I wrote that I am still having reverberations from all of the horrible things she said to me, and just don't feel safe. I apologized again for anything and everything I have done that has ever hurt her, and I thanked her for the offer, and I did all of the other nice things a daughter is supposed to do.

She wrote back: "Walk free, with my blessing."

November 8

I feel the inward turn today. I have no desire to do anything at all, other than eat, sleep, and dream. I have work to do and yet my brain does not cooperate. It wants only to lie here and contemplate the sky and the trees, to feel my baby move from side to side, to wonder about his face, his future.

November 10

Insomnia. My new bedtime is five a.m. I watch TV, read, scour the Internet for information about what the hell I am supposed to be doing and feeling this week. I worry. Can I really do this? What will become of me? Will I be trapped and miserable? I organize. I throw papers away, I order what I call "organizational principles" from the Container Store and make pretty, chronologically ordered file folders full of contracts, notes, articles, bills. I shred documents that I wouldn't want anyone else to see: medical records, first drafts, copies of tax returns.

I am up so much at night that it is starting to feel like day to me. Like I have collapsed the artificial line between day and night and I am living one long, seamless stream of life.

Another gift from Tenzin.

November 12

We nixed the postpartum-doula idea. We just don't want to have to deal with another person. I wish I could judge how incapacitated I will be. Some women I've talked to can't function for weeks and others get up after two days and do the grocery shopping. Where will I be on the spectrum? I have no idea. It all depends on the kind of birth I have.

In lieu of a doula, I figure I can get services lined up now so I won't worry about certain things. Like bottles of water. Fresh produce. Housecleaning.

Mr. T is moving around a lot today, kicking and elbowing me, his knees and tush sticking out from my belly. I started rubbing the parts that I can feel, massaging them and talking to him while I rubbed. He loved it.

November 19

We went to meet Sonam's backup doctor today, as required. When we arrived at her office in the Women's Center of the hospital, the small waiting room was packed with pregnant women about to pop. The doctors were running forty-five minutes to an hour late. There were no windows in the office, and the room was hot and stuffy.

To my left was a young woman ten days past her due date who kept shrieking, to no one in particular, It won't come out, it won't come out. She was accompanied by her mother, who looked stonily at the ground as her daughter moaned. At one point, this young woman asked another woman if her placenta was going to get stuck, and what she should do to make sure it comes out. The other woman very nicely told her not to worry, it would come out right after the baby.

There was a woman with a huge attitude talking on her cell phone to the father of her child. She told him that he needed to buy the baby some clothes or some formula since he hadn't done anything else for her the whole time she was pregnant. He said something and she said she didn't care about all that, all she knew was that he better buy something for this baby. Then she clicked her phone shut and went back to reading her magazine.

A young couple sat down next to us. They could have been in high school. The guy kept his arm around the girl the whole time we waited. She flipped through a magazine and they read it together, laughing sometimes, reading parts out loud to each other. Besides Glen, the guy was the only other man in a room full of hugely pregnant women.

About fifteen minutes before we were called in, a woman came in with her baby in a portable car seat. Turned out she was one of Sonam's patients. She said her birth went great, "You're gonna have a blast," which was the first time I had heard it put exactly like that. She also told me that it was all about the traveling car seat and that no, it wasn't too heavy.

I asked her how she was doing, and she said good. She tore a little bit, but it was all healed, and her energy was starting to come back. She said she was sweating all the time because her hormones were all over the place, and that nursing was harder than she thought it would be, but other than that she was loving being with her baby and it was all so much more normal and natural than she thought it would be.

Which was a relief.

Then the "It won't come out" woman asked her whether her placenta had come out on its own, or if she had to do something special to get it to come out, and the car-seat woman very patiently explained that no, you don't have to do anything special, it just comes out on its own after the baby. And the "It won't come out" woman nodded her head.

We were finally called in to meet with the doctor, who looked me over and said that for the most part everything looks fine and perfect and right on track, including the fact that I weigh 184 pounds. She said the low iron is still a problem. She's going to look into iron shots as a possibility but in the meantime told me to keep eating the beef, which I assured her I am, in copious amounts, thanks to Glen.

When she left the room, I started crying. It was just so intense in there. All those women. That young girl, probably developmentally disabled, not knowing what's going on. The tiny, airless office. Glen reminded me that we could be having the baby in the very nice, very airy hospital near our house. Which made me cry even harder.

November 24

I've started reading children's books. The Berenstain Bears, Richard Scarry, *Goodnight Moon*. The books take me back to purity, simplicity, ease. I remember why these books were my best friends when I was a little girl. Everything gets worked out, people love each other, the world is good.

I am reading these to counterbalance the e-mails that have been flying back and forth between me and my mother. I ask her to apologize for the dreaded afternoon and the statement she threatened to send to *Salon,* and to acknowledge the ways she has hurt me over the years with neglect, withholding, and the ambivalence she seems to have about my race, relative privilege, and birth itself.

She writes back that she has apologized enough and that children should forgive their parents and move on. She tells me that she and all of her friends think that because I have asked for this apology, I have lost my mind. I write her that asking people, even one's parents, to be accountable for their actions is the epitome of sanity, and that I am sorry that her friends, all of whom I know and love, don't have the courage to stand up to her.

When I write that if she can't apologize, I don't want contact because I feel she is too emotionally dangerous to me and my unborn son, she writes that she won't miss what we don't have and that to her our relationship has been inconsequential for years. She writes that she has been my mother for thirty years and is no longer interested in the job. Instead of signing "your mother" at the end of the letter, she signs her first name.

After that e-mail, I lie in bed trying to imagine some circumstance that could cause me to tell my child that I no longer want the job of being his mother. I think about Michael Jackson's mother, standing by his side in court as he responds to charges that he sexually molested children. I think about Scott Peterson's mother, who maintains that her son is a good boy even after he's been convicted of murdering his wife and child. Am I that awful, that I should no longer have a mother? Does telling my story the way I remember it make me a devil?

I try to imagine a circumstance that would lead me to tell my mother that I no longer want to be her daughter, that the job is just too draining, and I've found someone more suitable to take her place. When Glen walks in, I ask him to help me think, because, frankly, I am at a loss. I haven't even seen my baby and I feel I would die for him, kill for him if I had to. If I hurt him in some way, I imagine I would apologize to him over and over again until he could hear me, because that's what parents must do.

Glen sighs. It's not rational, honey, he says gently. An irrational person can find an endless number of reasons to justify ending a parent–child relationship, but a rational person knows that nothing can break that bond and it's madness to even try.

November 29

I am starting to think that giving the baby a Tibetan name isn't a betrayal of family as much as it is a sign of maturity.

Glen and I were flipping through a magazine, talking about how many people are stunted in their development, hovering in an adolescent state well into their fifties and sixties, even until death. He defined adolescence as being overly concerned with the acceptance of peers, and fearful of rejection or confrontation with the adult world.

Which made me think of how few people break away from the expectations of their parents to live their own, authentic lives. Guilt and fear keep so many of us ensnared. Who can stand the emotional blowback that comes from choosing a different path?

If guilt and fear keep us from acting on our own beliefs and aspirations, and not acting on our own beliefs and aspirations keeps us in a state of arrested development, there are bound to be some serious problems. If we aren't diligent in our efforts to mature, at some point cutting the cord of familial expectation, we become infantilized by it.

Sobering, but inescapable.

December 1

For research and recreation, I've been watching births on the Discovery Channel. It's amazing how many of these programs there are.

So far they fall into two categories:

The first is the normal birth. The mom lies calmly with her feet in the stirrups. She's completely epiduraled and everyone is just waiting, waiting, waiting until she's dilated. She looks content, and people come in and kiss her head and whisper in her ear. When it's showtime, the doctor comes in and peels back the sheet. He tells her to push. And push some more. Then we cut to commercial. Then we come back, and she's almost done. One more push, one more, there it is, yes! Congratulations, Samantha, you have a boy, a girl, a healthy baby. And everyone starts crying. If it's the home makeover show, this is when we cut to the almost-finished nursery, complete with gender-appropriate theme.

The second version is the complicated birth. In this segment, the mom does not look relaxed. She is on a gurney instead of a hospital bed. She looks panicked, in pain. She's practically crawling out of her skin. Doctors surround her and shout orders to nurses. Friends and family are remote. Then the decision to cut, to deliver by C-section.

Mom is rushed to the OR, where a sheet is thrown over her legs so she can't see what's about to happen. Seconds later a bloody infant is held up, followed by applause, relief, exhaustion. Mom gets to rest her cheek on the baby for a few seconds and then, before we can wonder about the gash in her belly, we go to commercial.

Glen says I shouldn't watch, that it's like watching movies about plane crashes before taking a trip. But I am compelled.

He doesn't understand that I am measuring myself against the women I'm watching, trying to convince myself that giving birth is something I can actually do. When I watch the normal births, I say things to myself like, If she can do it, I can do it. I am tougher than she is. Oh, for God's sake, that's a piece of cake. When I watch the births with complications, I think: *Oh my God, I am never going to make it.*

I want to see a home birth, a natural birth. I want to see what it looks like with no anesthesia and no emergency C-section. What channel is that on?

December 2

It finally hit me that all of this nesting, this obsession with the right bed, the right stroller, the right house, the right amount of money, is about trying to control an absolutely uncontrollable situation.

It's about fear.

It is all in lieu of the actual work, which is to prepare to give birth the way I must prepare to die: alone. This morning at four forty-nine I realized that I alone am having this baby. Glen and the midwife will be in the room, but no one can come and do this for me, no one can make it not be hard, no one can make it not hurt. No one can bear the pain so that I don't have to.

The notion of waiting for someone else to bear your burdens, to save you—pregnancy is a lesson in the futility of all of that.

I feel relief, as if a huge burden has been lifted and I can let go of the superficial aspects of this pregnancy.

I feel like an adult.

December 4

Woke up this morning after the long, detailed meeting with Sonam, Glen, and Natasha, the masseuse and birth assistant I chose to be my doula, full of energy. I made a big breakfast, cleaned the kitchen, worked on the textbook piece, drove Glen to a doctor's appointment, went out to lunch, and kept going until five. I didn't realize I was in an altered state until later, when it dawned on me that the odd tightening across my big belly was my first set of contractions.

At six, I had a primal urge to be as close to Glen as possible, preferably with my face buried in his armpit, but not before eating an entire chicken, a loaf of bread, and two bottles of mineral water. I know it seems like I am exaggerating, and when I read this in a year I'll be like, Yeah right. I am not exaggerating. I really did eat that much. Tenzin, you have always been a healthy, strong, strapping boy.

Then at about two a.m., I had another very strong urge to complete all of my outstanding work. So I finished the textbook pieces and e-mailed them to the editor, and made a detailed list of the rest of the work to wrap up. I taped it on the wall next to all the other lists I've been compiling, and finally, after I read all of them over, tumbled into bed.

I dreamed that I went to the bathroom and looked down and there was my "bloody show." When I thought, *Oh my God, it's happening,* the baby slid out of me, right into the toilet.

December 6

Tonight I lay in bed thinking about the scarcity model versus the abundance model. For my whole life, I have operated as though there isn't enough love to go around, that love is something that must be stockpiled, hoarded, guarded for fear of losing a few precious drops. But lately, maybe because I've been contemplating what life would be like if I had, gasp, two or even three children, I have been thinking about how, while there may never be enough time or money, there will always be enough love.

What if everyone could let go of the fear and territoriality that comes from trying to control the love supply? What if everyone realized that love is about giving, not getting? What if everyone realized all of these things before it was too late?

What if it is true that when you believe in abundance, what you have multiplies magically?

December 13

Tomorrow is D-day and I don't feel any different than I have felt for the last couple of weeks: huge, heavy, and hungry. I thought I would have a premonition, or a sense of imminent arrival, but I just feel like, la-di-da, I am a pregnant woman waiting for my baby, who may or may not arrive at any moment.

In the meantime, I continue to prepare. I called the hospital today and pre-registered. I washed, folded, and put away all of the baby clothes, including six receiving blankets, twenty white onesies, three of the cutest little shirts with giraffes and monkeys on them, two little cotton hats, and a rainbow of the teeniest socks.

In packing the bag for the hospital I realized I haven't handled the nursing-bra situation, so Glen and I went to the mall and let the very nice saleswoman sell us a few. I even got one to wear at night while I sleep, which I cannot imagine doing, but the saleswoman was so certain I will need it that I couldn't leave it behind.

When we got home, I continued packing, and watched *The King of Queens* as I worked. Carrie finds out she is pregnant and is terrified they don't have enough money or maturity to have a baby. Doug gets really excited and vows to carry the financial burden by taking a second job. Carrie shops for baby furniture, and encounters a salesperson who convinces her that she absolutely needs, must have, a seven-hundred-dollar changing table with a safety lip. Doug takes a job driving a limo and gets as his first passenger the owner of CBS, who he thinks is the owner of CVS, the pharmacy. He passes out at the gynecologist's office because Carrie's no longer his sexy wife Carrie, she's more like the model of the impregnated uterus. They talk, convince each other it's going to be great. Doug buys a receiving blanket and comes home to find Carrie in the would-be baby's room, depressed. She lost the baby.

Even though I knew it was going to happen because I've seen the whole next two seasons and they don't have a baby, I was still hit pretty hard. Glen came in to find me on the edge of the bed, crying. Again.

If something happens to this baby I don't think I will make it. No, really. I don't.

December 14

No sign of *el muchacho*. Sonam came over to check me. When she walked in she said, You look like a mother today. And I grinned, because today I feel like a mother. I don't know when or how it happened, but I definitely have crossed over into mommy-hood.

We talked about inducing. Whether we should, when we should, how we should. I don't want to rush him. I feel confident that he'll be right on time. On the other hand, I don't want to wait so long that it creates a problem. We came up with a plan: If he doesn't come by the twenty-second, we'll induce. He'll be a week late, which is still in the realm of healthy. In the meantime, Sonam gave me a list of natural ways to induce, including sex, crying, and eating black licorice. I pinned it on the wall next to all the other lists I've made in the last eight months: Iron-rich foods, things for the hospital, Five Best Things Your Partner Can Tell You When You're Pregnant.

Sonam also said that I must get more sleep. It's hard, though, because the baby wakes up at night and I'm right there with him. His body isn't moving, but I can feel his mind. He's being, listening, waiting.

December 16

I assembled the co-sleeper today. And then I stared at it for an hour, unable to imagine what it will feel like to have a real, live baby lying next to me at night.

I can see him now, not the details, but the blur of his face. And we've been talking to each other. Ready? Ready. Ready? Ready.

Today I caught myself singing to him. At first it was "Michael, Row Your Boat Ashore," and then it was both of the Color War alma maters that I can remember from summer camp, and then, I am embarrassed to even write this: "Kumbaya." But I sang that one only because I couldn't think of any other songs besides "You

Are the Sunshine of My Life," "You've Got a Friend," "Isn't She Lovely," and "Let's Stay Together."

How is it possible that I don't know any lullabies? My father's friend George gave me ten CDs of lullabies from all over the world. Obviously, every other woman on the planet has lullabies welling up naturally from the depths of her soul. Why don't I have a whole repertoire, in multiple languages? When I asked Glen he said, I don't recall the baby asking you to sing him a medley of lullabies from around the world.

Which is true, and made me laugh.

People have been calling every day now that I am past the due date. Is he here? How are you doing? Sweet to feel them in the space with me: waiting, waiting, waiting.

Eight

I FIRST MET GLEN at a meditation retreat. I was tearing through a plate of organic greens and tofu lasagna in the dining room of the retreat center when I turned my head slightly and caught sight of him. He was three empty chairs away, and wore the burgundy robes of a Buddhist tradition I didn't recognize. He had a full beard, large hands, and soft brown eyes.

Ordinarily I would have turned away, but because we were up in the mountains with only each other and sixty or so others for company, I did not. I smiled when our eyes met and paused, taking him in. He too was quiet, not rushing to fill the space. Then in the least intrusive but most penetrating voice I've ever heard, he said hello. I gave a slight bow. Hello. And then we didn't speak for the rest of the meal.

I saw him next the following morning, at the early teaching.

I was groggy from lack of sleep, but I noticed Glen right away when I walked into the meditation hall. He was sitting off to the side, looking at and seemingly through the entire group of assembled students. He was purposefully threading a thick, rose-colored *mala* through his fingers. He was so still he was practically invisible.

That morning, I listened respectfully to the teaching, but really I was already attuned to Glen, and found myself glancing over at him several times during the two-hour session. When it was finally his turn to teach, I felt a curious mixture of excitement and readiness. This is a cliché, but when he began to speak, I really did feel as though he was speaking only to me. When he sang a *doha,* an ancient song calling all beings to enlightenment, I wept.

A year later we sat in a Japanese restaurant. We had not been out of contact for more than a day since the afternoon in the dining room. As is customary in the teacher–student relationship in the Vajrayana tradition, Glen had committed himself to transmitting to me some of the most esoteric of Buddhist teachings, and I had committed to deepening my devotion to him in order to receive them. As is customary in the romantic tradition of modernity, as my lover Glen had committed himself to making me happy and I had almost committed to letting him.

I was open but a bit unsure. I had heard horrible stories about teachers and students who became involved. There were messy, public lawsuits, and whole websites devoted to documenting incidents of "sexual misconduct." Family members expressed concern. I listened, but ultimately had to acknowledge that in the midst of so much doubt, no one could deny that I was happier than I had ever been. In one year, I had healed relationships that had been broken for decades, and jettisoned relationships that had no possibility of coming around. My work was more satisfying. I fired my therapist. I smiled more in one day after meeting Glen than I had in a whole year before.

And he wanted to have a baby.

I had told him shortly after our meeting just like I had told everybody else: *I want to have a baby.* But unlike everyone else, he responded decisively. Of course you want to have a baby, he said, and you should. There are things you learn when you have a baby that you cannot learn any other way. You find out what life is about when you carry another human being in your womb. You find out what really matters when you straddle life and death to push your child through the birth canal.

I told him about my list of potential daddy donors, about Ade. I told him about the abortion I had when I was fourteen and my fear that I would not be able to conceive. I told him about Solomon. We talked about the years I had spent running from potential mates and devoting my life to people completely unsuited.

We talked for hours every day, and it was as if the years slid off me with each conversation. Self-concepts were reevaluated. The constant loop of self-deprecation that had been running in my head for decades grew less and less audible. When Glen wondered why I didn't listen more attentively to my ten-year longing, I asked myself the same question. What would it mean for me to have a baby? What would the experience reveal? Why did I crave it so profoundly? After several months, I began to wake up in the morning believing that having a child was not only possible, but necessary.

One day in my icebox of a writing studio by the sea, I told Glen of a dream I had been having for several years. There was a little boy, sleeping in a cave, and there was an angry woman, stabbing at my heart. The boy was waiting patiently for me to come, and the woman was trying to prevent me from getting there.

Glen stood in front of a huge panel of my printed pages thumbtacked to the wall in a neat row of white rectangles, nodding as I described the colors in the dream, the sound of the knife slicing through the air. When he finally did say something, he didn't so much decipher the dream as join me in the labyrinth of it.

He wondered if my happiness was dangling in the space between the boy and the woman trying to keep me from him. Who was she and how could I get past her? Who was he? On reflection, it occurred to me that this boy curled up in the invisible space around my body could be *my* boy. He slept peacefully, patiently, as if he knew for certain that I would come. As if he knew that I would slay the dragon and vanquish the enemy, that the fight would end and we, he and I, would win.

This little boy knew what I was only just beginning to suspect. That with Glen I was healing something that had been broken for a very long time: my ability to trust, my right to dream. I was repairing my broken faith, but it was far from restored. Which is why I laughed nervously into my tempura udon when Glen told me that I had found the father of my child and could stop looking.

I was thirty-three. I had been considering having a baby for more than ten years. I had finally met someone who was willing and able to give me the partnership I craved. I was in love, and I was scared to death. Scared of closing an unseen, imaginary door by walking through the open one in front of me. Terrified of following a vision that had beckoned for more than a decade.

Could I even take care of a child? When I looked back, there were so many broken relationships, stories that started out shiny and happy just like this one. But now there would be a vulnerable child in the balance.

As if reading my mind, Glen suggested that the healing would come through my not doing to my child what was done to me. Not succumbing to divorce. Not forcing my child to adapt to wildly divergent circumstances to suit my lifestyle. Not arguing. Not making him hold the unresolved issues of the generations that preceded him. Not forcing him to choose which parent to believe, to trust, to become.

If I could do this on behalf of my actual child and the neglected child inside of myself, the demon would have no choice but to put down her knife. My child would awaken and live. I would know how to protect myself. The cutter, the mutilator, would not be allowed inside.

I knew Glen was right, but I was also frightened of making a conscious decision, a reasoned choice. I had lived my life tumbling headlong into scenarios, captivated by ideas like fate and romantic love. What did it mean to decide, after extensive evaluation and discussion, to move forward together, instead of waking up one morning to realize that yet another boundary had been crossed and I was now deeper into a relationship that I really did not fully understand?

I loved Glen deeply. But because I was with him engaged in the project of giving up drama forever, our relationship was disturbingly stable, calm, rational. When I told my father about Glen, he said that our relationship sounded good but that something was missing. We were walking arm in arm around the lake in Central Park. It's clear that you love this person, he said, stopping by one of the benches. But Rebecca, tell me, are you in love with him?

At the time, I brushed it off. In love? I've been in love, and where has that gotten me? We laughed, but my mind seized on the question as we navigated the throngs on Fifth Avenue. I've met a man who has brought me more happiness than I imagined possible, who has offered to give me the one experience I've craved my whole life, who has stood by my side through depths of despair so profound I was afraid to mention them for fear of shattering your faith in yourself as a parent, and you ask if I am in love with him?

Loving, being in love. The whole idea of a difference between the two suddenly struck me as preposterous. And yet, if I wasn't intoxicated, swept off my feet, was I settling? Was I like other women who had reached a certain age—in my case, thirty-three—and found themselves in need of a certain sperm donor daddy type? Was Glen just a prudent and convenient choice?

This was the voice of the woman with the machete. Always slashing to bits whatever piece of happiness I managed to find. Was she my mother? This was the voice of my father's pervasive ambivalence, transmitted from one generation to the next through innocent conversations like the one in the park.

I slurped my noodles.

I put the woman's own knife to her neck and bade her farewell.

I leapt with certainty into the void.

Nine months later, I was pregnant.

LIKE ALL COUPLES, Glen and I have gone over that first hello a thousand times. We've marveled at how, of all the people present, we ended up next to each other, with empty seats and not obscuring human bodies in between. We've excavated the back story: Glen hadn't planned to go to lunch at all that day, but changed his mind and turned into the dining room instead. I hadn't planned to go to the retreat at all, but changed my mind and drove myself the seventy-five miles from the city.

At the retreat, though joined by a common interest in Buddhism, we were in distinctly different camps. I was with a group of women practitioners who visited the retreat center regularly and had for many years. He had never been on the property and was there because his students, most of whom were men, had implored the head teachers to invite him. With a word, we breached the space between territories and created a whole new world, separate and distinct from both.

Are we reading too much into it? Perhaps. But I have yet to meet a couple that didn't feel the echoes of destiny, fate, angels, or, as Buddhists call it, karma. Buddhists don't believe in a god up in heaven moving people around like chess pieces across the universe. But we do believe in cause and effect: that each moment is very much the result of all the moments that came before.

In one cosmic moment, we stepped into the stream of our son's potential for being. We decided to say hello, and the rest, as they say, is history.

Or Tenzin's story.

December 20

I wrote the baby a note this morning, thinking he might need a little reassurance.

> Dearest baby,
>
> Hi, sweetheart. It's time for you to come out of Mommy's stomach. I know it is all cushy and warm in there and you are enjoying all your favorite foods, but I promise you'll like it out here, too. Mommy and Daddy love you and we can't wait to see you and kiss you and take care of you.
>
> Don't be afraid. Mommy hasn't done this before, either, but I know we can do it! We'll do it together.
>
> Love,
> Mommy

December 21

I feel as if we have all merged. Glen, the baby, and I have become one unit. I've gone from one to three.

Tonight I feel ready. I give. I surrender. I know it's completely beyond my control.

There is nothing for me to do except let go and let it happen.

Do you hear me, little one? I'm waving the white flag. Do your thing.

I'll be there.

December 22

He's here!

But may I ask one small but very relevant question? Why the hell didn't anyone tell me how much it was going to hurt? The only thing that could ease that pain was an *epidural,* and if I do this again, which at the moment I cannot imagine, I will demand one after the first contraction, if not before.

The whole thing was a miracle, but more on that later. At the moment I must document my newfound respect for every human being that has given birth, and I retract my judgment of every woman who has had or will have a scheduled C-section. Maybe I just have a low threshold for pain, but I don't think so. It is *outrageous.* I remember screaming, somewhere in between the toilet, the birthing pool, the bed, and the shower, that I couldn't believe every person on this earth got here this way. It just doesn't seem possible.

But it is, and now, thirty hours after it all began, I have a little baby boy who is undeniably the most precious being I have ever seen.

I honestly don't know if I can bear it.

His name is Tenzin Walker.

Suffice it to say, all is not peaches and cream. Tenzin is in the neonatal intensive care unit, but I am too exhausted to write the entire saga, so it will have to wait until tomorrow.

December 23

The Entire Saga:

Yesterday at five o'clock I was so hungry I felt I could eat the headboard off my new bed. Glen brought me what I craved: quick, greasy take-out that I ate with abandon. A huge hamburger with onions, bacon, and cheddar cheese, a Greek salad, and two orders of french fries disappeared within minutes.

At seven, I was checking e-mail and noticed the vivid purple and red streaks of the sunset outside my window. I felt relieved that I had cleared all the writing assignments from my desktop. I went to the bathroom and saw a little blood, not a clot, but enough to think that something might be happening. I called Glen and then Sonam, who asked if there was a lot of fluid. I said no and she said it may be starting, but maybe not. She told me to breathe, stay calm, and keep in touch.

I made it to the bed before the first contraction hit. It was like the contractions I had been having except this one extended beyond my belly deep into my pelvis. It was slightly orgasmic, and I thought that if this was it I couldn't imagine why anyone would want to have an epidural. Then the contractions started coming every ten minutes or so, with growing intensity. After forty-five minutes, I could no longer sit still. I asked Glen if this was it, was it happening, and he said, Could be, but let's just stay calm and wait and see.

He got a little pad out and started taking notes, and I got really upset. Of course, I was writing cryptic messages to myself in my tiny blue notebook, but him doing the same thing made me feel like an animal under observation. I got pissy and he said I was trying to control his experience. I had a flash of depression: Were we really going to have an argument as I was going into labor?

No.

Once he put the notebook away, labor took off like a rocket and I couldn't hold on to any thoughts at all. The contractions started coming faster. There was a two- or three-minute break between them, but after the first minute, I dreaded the coming of the next one and began to clench in anticipation.

I called Sonam again and told her how fast they were coming. She said it sounded like I was in labor and she was going to pack her bag and come over. The pain started to get super-intense. I had a strong urge to take off all my clothes and lie in the bed with Glen until it was all over, but the only way I could survive the contractions was to keep getting up and sitting down. Then one of them hit and hurt so much that I fell to my knees. I spent the next two hours going from the floor of the bathroom to the toilet.

Sonam arrived and found me on all fours on the bathroom floor. She checked me and said that I was completely effaced and already a few centimeters dilated. She said we should get ready to go to the hospital. I didn't think I could get to the front door, let alone the hospital, and I think I screamed that out, along with some other unsavory epithets.

Glen swung into high gear, getting the food bags and my hospital bag and my coat and blankets and pillows covered with garbage bags in case my water broke in the car. I kept calling for him and he kept coming back to the bathroom every few minutes to tell me he was getting everything ready and that now was the time to execute our plan, not rethink it. Which would have made more sense to me if I could have executed getting off the bathroom floor.

From somewhere far, far away, I think the living room, I heard Sonam call Natasha and tell her that we would be at the hospital within the hour and she should go over and start setting up the birthing pool. That sounded so reasonable, but it also sounded like Sonam and Glen were both completely out of touch with reality. In between contractions, I told them so in a conversation I had with them in my mind. In our little imaginary chat, I told them that there was no way I could leave the bathroom floor, and we should prepare to have the baby in the bathtub. I had plenty of towels and there was a toilet and a shower and they were both there and, well, what more could we possibly need?

But then Glen and Sonam were helping me up and leading me to the car, and I was grabbing all kinds of random things like scarves and little bottles of massage oil and my favorite socks with the anti-skid patches on the bottom and several notebooks until Glen cut through it all and said, Rebecca, we have to go right now. And I thought, *Okay, got it. I can't back out of this, I can't procrastinate, I've got to just get with the program and get my ass in the car.* Then we were in the car and speeding along in the dark and I literally thought I was going to die. The contractions were coming in waves and the pain was so intense and unbearable I couldn't do anything but scream and freak out and lose my mind when they hit.

Which is what I was doing when we drove up to the emergency room and a security guard offered to get me a wheelchair. I said no, thanks, and then he asked again, directing his question to Glen and

I almost tore his head off. I don't want a wheelchair, I screamed. Just open the door and tell me where to go.

I don't remember being in the elevator but I do remember Natasha coming down and getting all of our bags and I remember getting to the room and throwing myself onto the futon. After a few minutes, the contractions forced me to my hands and knees and I started crawling around screaming that I couldn't believe all human beings came here this way and that every single mother had to go through this.

Sonam and Natasha were calm and trying to help, but it was not at all like I thought it would be, with soft lights and my aromatherapy atomizer spritzing lavender-scented negative ions into the room and Natasha rubbing my back and Glen whispering in my ear and Sonam directing nurses and giving me visualizations. It was chaos and mayhem, and there was no room in the experience for anyone but me. I asked Natasha to rub my feet and arms and legs, and she tried for about forty seconds before I ran to the toilet and then decided that what I wanted—no, *desperately needed*—was to take a shower.

Glen turned the water on and stood with me while I gripped the safety rail, lay my head on the plastic wall, and wailed that I didn't think I could make it. Then I got into the birthing pool, the thing I thought would be my salvation, and it was, for about ten minutes. Then it got too hot and I couldn't move around enough so I had to get up and go back to the bathroom.

By this point it must have been one or two in the morning and we had been going since eight. I got up on the bed and hit the toilet a few more times and then Sonam checked me and said I was about four centimeters and we needed to get to eight, and that's when I realized there was no way I could do it. I was exhausted and it hurt so fucking much and I just couldn't believe that I had so much more to endure. I looked at Natasha, Sonam, and Glen standing respectfully at the periphery of my experience, in it with me, but only as far as they could be. Then I said, really loud, *I want an epidural.*

The three of them looked at each other, not sure what to do. Looking into their blank faces, I reminded them that I asked them to get me an epidural if I wanted it. They started to deliberate, and then to try and talk me out of it. At which point I began to plead for the epidural. Please, you guys, don't make me beg. Just get me the epidural. I have got to have the epidural. Please go get me the epidural.

The moment Sonam went to get the anesthesiologist, I started to feel better. It still hurt like bloody hell, but I knew it was going to end and that gave me a moment's respite from the horrifying thought that I was going to be in this god-awful pain forever. The sun started to come up and the room got very still, punctuated by me screaming at anyone who entered the room: Are you the anesthesiologist? Get the anesthesiologist. When is the anesthesiologist coming? Where is the anesthesiologist?

I have never been as happy to see another human being as I was when the anesthesiologist walked over to my bed and told me to sit up so that she could insert the epidural. I was almost weeping with gratitude. She introduced herself and told me what to expect and I felt a stick and some jostling at the base of my spine and heard some tape being pulled from a tape dispenser. The nurses were talking to each other but I started to lose track of what they were saying, and slowly, slowly the pain began to lessen until I was relaxing in an extremely pleasant haze, and Glen was rubbing my forehead and telling me to take a break and get some rest.

That was lovely.

I floated in and out of consciousness for a while, and everyone took a breather because I was calm and not crawling around like a madwoman. Glen called my father and left messages for a few friends. Sonam got some juice. Natasha rubbed my feet and fluffed my pillows. The nurse had me breathe some extra oxygen and told me I was doing great. Then, just as I was really getting into it, and thinking I was finally going to be able to get some sleep, Sonam checked me and said that I was fully dilated and it was time to push. She said it might be hard to feel the contractions because of the epidural, but that I was going to have to really focus and try my best.

Even though I didn't want to go back to work, I was game to push because I thought that meant I was almost done. After what I had just gone through, how hard could pushing be? I got up on my elbows and grabbed Glen's hand and started giving it my all, bearing down and grunting and straining and making hideous faces, none of which had any effect whatsoever. I couldn't feel anything below my waist. The baby wasn't moving, but Sonam did see that he was posterior, turned around, which was going to make everything even harder.

Right around this time, when Sonam was telling me that a shot of Pitocin would intensify the contractions and make pushing easier, the nurse started getting adamant about the oxygen. The numbers coming out of her machine were not good, and suggested the baby was going into distress. His heart rate was down, which meant he wasn't getting enough oxygen. I could tell that she was a little concerned, but trying to make it sound totally normal so I wouldn't fall apart. This was not effective. I believe I started to say "What is wrong with the baby?" over and over again and when they told me, I tried to take in the oxygen, but the mask was so awkward and uncomfortable that it was hard for me to push, worry, and breathe at the same time. The Pitocin started to kick in and so did the pain. I pushed and pushed until I couldn't stand it anymore and then Sonam went to find the anesthesiologist to top off my epidural.

At that point, time began to be a major issue. The nurse's machine was beeping and she kept putting the oxygen over my face and doctors started coming into the room to see what was going on and provide backup. I was making a little headway with the pushing, but not much. The baby would come out a little and then go back. He did that several times, until I was completely exhausted and didn't think I could do any more. That was when I started saying, Just cut me open and get the baby.

Then he made it out a little farther, but got caught under my pelvic bone on the right side. Which hurt like hell, in addition to all the other hurting like hell going on. Then he and I did the "Okay, let's get you out from under my pubic bone" dance for what seemed like an eternity. I was pushing so hard I thought the sides of my head were going to burst open. I was pushing so hard I thought I was going to knock myself unconscious. I was pushing so hard and I still couldn't feel the baby coming out.

The room was filling up with people but I couldn't focus on who they might be or why they were there. Sonam's backup doctor came in completely covered in OR blues and stood very close to me, speaking directly into my ear. She said, The baby is in distress. If you can't get the baby out in the next few pushes, we are going to have to do a C-section. Do you understand what I am saying? I looked at Glen and he was stable and calm, and then I heard Sonam tell the doctor that she knew I could do it. She is definitely going to get this baby out, she said.

The only thing I could think to do was get on my hands and knees and try to get him out that way. Sonam was yelling, Push your baby out, Rebecca. Bring your baby into the world, Rebecca. Come on, push. I could feel all the people in the room watching, suspended in the moment. I had a flash that I should feel embarrassed about being naked on my hands and knees in front of a room full of strangers, but honestly, I couldn't have cared less. Really. It was more like, I hope they understand that they are experiencing a goddamn miracle right now. It doesn't get more real than this.

Then time opened up, the seconds expanded into a dozen dimensions, and everybody in the room fell into it. At the exact moment I thought I was going to collapse and be wheeled into the OR and cut open, I felt the baby's head pop free and Sonam said, That's it, one more big push, one more, come on. And I pushed and then he was slithering out of my body and everyone in the room broke into applause and I started crying and fell back onto the bed.

People were making all kinds of oohing sounds and Sonam said, You did it! You had a healthy vaginal birth! Then she asked if Glen wanted to cut the umbilical cord. Glen said yes and took the scissors and did a blessing over the baby in Tibetan. With one snip, me and my boy went from one to two. Sonam placed him on my chest and the two of us lay there together, exhausted.

He was breathing heavily and looking around with calm curiosity. I couldn't see him so much as feel him, his slippery, smooth torso and floppy limbs. And his mind, I felt his perfectly open and clear mind. He was so present, so unencumbered by ideas about what he was seeing that I felt I was holding a being from another planet.

Then they took him away from me and I started to hear doctors mumbling about meconium and they asked Glen to go with them to the NICU and then I was just lying there, with a gaping hole in my belly and no baby in my arms. Sonam sewed me up and I went to the NICU in a wheelchair to find my baby.

When I arrived at the NICU, the nurses brought me over to Tenzin. I almost broke down. He was completely naked, strapped under an oxygen tent with tubes and monitor leads coming out of his arms and legs. He looked cold, even though there was a warmer over him. The right side of his face was bruised, and skin was peeling off all over his body. His breathing was so labored that his chest and neck lifted off of the table each time he took a breath. I couldn't touch him because he couldn't come out of the tent, but I got close to the plastic cover and told him that Mommy was right there and he didn't have to worry and he'd be better soon.

He didn't move. I thought I was going to pass out. The word "agony" doesn't begin to capture what I felt.

Because the neonatologist wasn't there yet, the only thing I could do was talk to the nurse assigned to him and try to forge a bond. I hoped that my love and concern would be transmitted through her to the baby. Then I went to my little hospital room filled with unopened bags of stuff I thought was so essential to labor and passed out.

Four or five hours later, one of the neonatologists, Dr. Morales, came into our room. She said that Tenzin has meconium, the first waste product of the baby, in his lungs and that is making it hard for him to breathe in enough oxygen. He's getting oxygen now under the tent, and they've started him on a round of antibiotics to ward off infection. She said he is very vigorous, and has a very strong cry, which is a good sign. She said that babies with meconium are usually in the hospital for a week to ten days. She said we just have to watch him and hope the meconium cycles through and that he will be able to breathe on his own soon.

December 24

There are three neonatologists here who rotate. We met the second today. Turns out he is the father of an old college classmate, which is vaguely comforting.

Anyway. Dr. Thompson came into my room and we had a long talk. He thinks Tenzin had meconium in his lungs before he was even born, and that once he began to breathe, it corrupted the lung tissue. He said there was no meconium in the amniotic fluid so they didn't realize that he needed to be intubated at birth. I wanted to say no, it wasn't that there wasn't meconium in the fluid. There was no fluid. My water didn't break at all, probably because Tenzin was further past term than any of us thought and should have been induced.

But I didn't say that and instead just tried to listen to him without panicking. He described the meconium as tarlike and extremely noxious. If Tenzin breathed it in for several minutes, which he must have because he was on me for at least that long, there may be some lung damage. He says it is unlikely, and usually babies with meconium aspiration syndrome (MAS) go home after their time in the NICU breathing normally and have no long-term effects. He said the X ray shows that the right side is more "involved" than the left, which makes sense because that was the side that was hurting so much during labor, the side that got hooked under my pelvic bone.

I am able to process what the doctors tell me about Tenzin, but I must be in shock because that is all I can do. I can't believe how hard the labor was and how unprepared I was for it after all of that preparation. I can't believe he's in the NICU. I can't believe I am not nursing my baby right now, bathed in the idyllic glow of post-partum. Instead, I feel like I've been in a car accident.

I went online and put in "in utero meconium aspiration." The first listing that came up was "in utero meconium aspiration: an unpreventable cause of neonatal death."

THERE WILL BE no neonatal death on my watch.

Janet the breastfeeding consultant brought me a big yellow breast pump today. Even though I've gone over breastfeeding on the antidepressant a dozen times with Marie, Dr. Lowen, Sonam, and anyone else who would listen, I had to get another opinion from Janet, who referred to a book she whipped out of her pocket that says that the benefits outweigh the risk. I revved up the pump and got to work. Just a little colostrum, but it was enough to put in a bottle and take over to the NICU to store in the fridge. Storing food for the babe. Check.

December 25

Babies are flying through the NICU today. Every couple of hours there is a new "Jesus" or "Christopher" from the mostly Catholic moms. A volunteer group knits hats for the newborns, and so the baby Jesuses are lying in their plastic bassinets with tiny green and red caps on. Christmas isn't my thing, so I picked a nice beige one for Tenzin when his nurse, Rose, offered. Rose is from the Philippines and is very auntie-like. She talks to Tenzin in a singsongy voice, very loud, which seems to get his attention, and assures me he's going to be fine when I stare at him with longing and worry.

Tonight was better than last night, primarily because they've taken the oxygen tent away and given him a cannula that threads around his head, so at least he's not like the boy in the bubble. I can touch his forehead and rub my nose against his cheek. His breathing is still extremely labored, but so far everyone tells me he's quite vigorous for a baby as sick as he is, a good sign.

I was supposed to go home today, but Sonam managed to get me an extension, and then the hospital offered me a room for after that. They have a rooming-in policy for moms with sick babies. I can have a room close to the NICU as long as they don't need it for an incoming mom. I feel such gratitude for this humane policy, and wonder if the fancy, more expensive hospital has a similar policy. I don't know what I would do if I had to leave him every day. I don't think I could survive it.

December 26

It's two a.m. and I think I am having a nervous breakdown. I paged Natasha 911, and when she called I told her everything and she said it's all normal. Most women crash around day three postpartum. It's when all the feel-good hormones you've been carting around with the baby inside suddenly plummet, never to be seen or heard from again. I cannot wake Glen up again with another string of woes, but really, I feel unfit to be a mother, and that I failed at giving birth. If I hadn't been so pigheaded about natural childbirth, I might have known that he was late and had him induced, and then we might not be going through this. I refuse to beat myself up, and then I start swinging.

If all that wasn't enough, I hurt in so many inconvenient places it is ridiculous. I can't walk a step without feeling like my uterus is going to fall on the floor, and my lower back, where the epidural went in, is *killing* me. I could take a Vicodin to take the edge off, but the pain doesn't seem intense enough to justify passing a narcotic on to the baby. Sonam's backup midwife checked me this morning and reminded me that this is the kind of back pain that makes epidurals problematic. I didn't say anything, but I thought I would have to be damn near paralyzed to think twice about having another epidural. As far as I am concerned, that needle saved my life.

I am completely sick of dealing with blood and urine and shit and milk. It's like my whole body has been reduced to a quintet of oozing sores. And where is my baby? Where is my baby? Where is my baby?

I COULDN'T TAKE IT. I had to be near him, so I went over to the NICU and watched him sleep. His vulnerability is heartbreaking, practically unbearable. I don't understand how human beings have survived these feelings for millions of years. How mothers have survived losing their sons to war, losing their daughters to marriage and relocation, and how parents have survived losing their children to disease and famine.

When I was in my twenties, my mother told me that she had to decide to love me, that she could have gone either way and she *chose* to love me. At the time, her words seemed strange, but I had no reference point so I just nodded and felt grateful that she'd made the choice that didn't leave me motherless. Seeing Tenzin's vulnerability makes me shake my head in wonder at her disclosure. There is no choice involved in my love for Tenzin, and if there were some secret place where I wondered, and there isn't, I would never tell him about it.

What I will tell Tenzin one day is that his need for me and my love for him are by far the most powerful human truths I have ever known. I would give my life for his in a heartbeat, and in some ways I think that is what is happening. Giving birth *was* like dying and being reborn. I went into labor one person, and came out two. I went into labor with a singular consciousness, and came out with a consciousness that transcended my own. I understand now the Tantric teachings on giving birth to your enlightened mind, and why the feminine is exalted in those teachings. Women can literally give birth and, through this process, birth an expanded understanding, a more enlightened, transpersonal view.

I thought there would be loss and mourning involved in the abandonment of my preoccupation with myself, but so far, even with the unbelievable pain and complications, it is all gain. I feel lighter, clearer about what needs to be done, and what my role is in the whole big, astonishing universe. Tenzin is my son and I am his mother. Is there anything else?

December 27

I am feverish today, sweating and shivering. My breastfeeding book says it could be milk fever, which makes sense because my breasts are like giant gourds. Really. They are outrageously, obscenely engorged, painful to touch, and just, I don't know, so intense. When I walk, it's like I am a pair of breasts walking with a body attached. They lead when we enter a room, demanding acknowledgment and respect from all who come near.

Did I mention that they hurt?

I started pumping a couple of days ago, when Janet told me to store the colostrum, but today the floodgates have opened. I am now pumping every couple of hours, and filling bottles and bottles of milk. If I don't pump, I leak until I am drenched. Every time I walk over to the NICU to put another bottle in the fridge, one of the nurses says, Another one?

So here I am, scribbling this as I sit on the edge of the bed with my breasts stuck into mechanized suction cups strapped to my body with an elastic pumping bra. I feel like a cow, but every time I fill up another bottle I have a brief moment of ecstasy. My body is producing food for my baby. It doesn't get much better than that. Well, maybe it does. I'd rather be nursing. That would make a great bumper sticker to stick on this pump.

I'd rather be nursing. Yeah.

December 28

Not good. Tenzin is not improving and we have moved on to check for other possible diagnoses. Roth ordered a cardiac echo, which will check to make sure the valves in his heart are working properly and that the one that is supposed to have closed by now has done so.

That was sobering news. I settled in a little more after hearing that. When I was thinking we'd be going home in a week, I was more transient, mentally, but now it could be weeks.

I've moved into a new room because Labor and Delivery filled up and they needed my old one. This room is pretty rustic and has a mysterious leak in the floor. Getting out of bed this morning, I stepped in a huge puddle. After I told the nurse, a very nice man came to mop the water up, but within fifteen minutes the water was back. Then the engineer came up and said he couldn't figure out where the water was coming from. I told him I don't really care about the water, I just want to be close to my baby.

I unpacked the rest of my stuff here in the new room: food and robes and slippers and shirts and salves and medicines and baby clothes I thought Tenzin would be wearing by now. I burst into tears, and then I briefly considered going online. Friends and family have been calling and writing, but I don't have the energy to keep them abreast of what's happening. I need to keep my mind clear and focused on being there for the baby.

December 29

I am starting to feel closer to the nurses, especially Gemma and Rose, and I've struck up a friendship with another mom. I don't know her name, but her baby was born two months premature the day before Tenzin. This is her fourth child, and she's already up and back to work. She comes in the evenings to give the baby a bottle, sometimes with her husband. When she arrives, I give her whatever update I can. Like if her little girl was peaceful or ate a lot. And she asks if Tenzin is getting better. Did he gain weight? Have they lowered the oxygen? Then we sit there, not more than five feet between us, staring at our babies and willing them to be okay.

Gemma told me today that she was born in the Philippines and then went to work as a nurse in Dubai, where she met her Surinamese husband. They have two kids, a boy and a girl. The boy had meconium and is now totally fine, with no residual problems. She showed me a picture of him as proof. He's beautiful. Her little girl is three months old. She said she's jealous of all my milk (One of the nurses joked that they need a whole fridge just for Mommy Walker!) because she is pumping at work and not getting much, only three or four ounces. I can get out three ounces in three minutes.

We talked about how difficult it is to work full-time and raise two kids. She thought America would be different, but she has to work so much to pay for her mortgage and for the kids' schools. She said the quality of life was much better in Dubai (!). It is interesting to hear about the American Dream through the prism of her life. So far, I think she's my favorite nurse. She brings me ice water when I get to the NICU and tells me to get more rest, which I appreciate. Just that little bit of empathy helps so much.

I don't know what I will do if Tenzin has a heart problem. I am trying not to blame myself, or to feel like I've failed somehow. Was it something I ate? Should I have gone to the "better" hospital? I never should have left Dr. Lowen. Glen tells me not to beat myself up, but when I see Tenzin lying there alone, or when I walk into the NICU and hear him screaming his heart out as doctors and nurses walk right by, it's almost impossible. Even if no one is to blame, still, someone has to show up and take responsibility. Someone has to apologize over and over, and hold him until he knows that, at the very least, it's not *his* fault.

December 30

We've been struggling with the breastfeeding. Tenzin has a good latch, but it is clearly difficult for him to breathe and nurse at the same time.

Now when he cries and wants to be fed, the nurses call me on the phone at two a.m., five a.m., eight a.m., eleven. Mommy Walker! Your baby is crying. Will you please come to feed him? I hear Tenzin screaming at the top of his lungs in the background and I leap out of bed, throw on my robe, and run over to give him some milk.

He drinks a little and then chokes, coughs, turns his head away. Between his breathing difficulty and the incredible amount of milk streaming out of my breasts, it might just be too much. My breast-feeding book says that too much milk can overwhelm the baby and turn him off the breast completely. I spoke to Janet and she thinks I should stop pumping so often, to slow down the flow.

Now I'm anxious about traumatizing my baby with my breast milk! Glen thinks the bottle is the most manageable solution, but every time he suggests it I feel irrationally defensive. Last night I got really upset. I've already lost my postpartum bliss moment, I cried, now you want me to give up nursing, too? I am just so afraid we won't bond, or that he won't get what he needs, which is closeness with his mommy.

This afternoon a social worker came in to talk to us. I think she was trying to find out if there were any problems in our family like domestic abuse or drug addiction. She asked some very personal questions about our home life and told us about government programs we could apply for. Glen told me it was normal for the social worker to be available because the hospital is public and serves people who need help. She becomes their liaison.

I am glad of that, but she gave me the creeps. She started to give us a lecture on how different things were going to be with the baby and how we needed to prepare ourselves emotionally. I was like, Are you kidding?

I understand that people need services, but there was something not right about the approach, the assumptions made. Or maybe I just really want to go home with my baby and I am projecting my dissatisfaction onto the social worker.

THE TRUTH IS, I am obscenely jealous of the mothers who have problem-free births. Their babies just hit the NICU to be cleaned off, weighed, and measured, and then it's right back up to mom. I caught myself today looking enviously at those babies and feeling sorry for myself and Tenzin.

December 31

The cardiac echo came back normal today. Whoopeee! He has been taken off fluids and is now just getting breast milk. He's finally gaining weight and Dr. Morales says he's looking good. Still not healing as fast as he should, but the fact that he's gained a few ounces is encouraging.

I needed the good news. Last night I beat myself up for hours for staying on the antidepressant; for being half in the medical model and half in the midwifery model; for being so consumed with my big ideas that something bad happened to my pure, innocent, faultless baby.

After Dr. Morales told me the good news, I walked the hospital halls drenched in relief. Where else could I go? Last night as I was agonizing over the barely detectable traces of antidepressant found in breast milk, Glen told me that I am too hard on myself. He's right. Cruising through the different wards, I decided that I'm just like every other mother. I want to do the right thing, but sometimes life doesn't work out the way I've planned.

January 1

Passed a quiet New Year's Eve in the NICU, holding Tenzin and looking into his inquisitive brown eyes. Already, in the brief moments he is actually awake, he studies everything about me. He is getting to know my outer terrain like he knew the inner one. When I walk through the glass door of the NICU, all I have to do is say loudly in his direction that I have arrived. He stops crying immediately and waits patiently for me to wash my hands. Then we do our ritual of getting the pillow right, and my glass of water within reach, and the little stool under my feet. I lift him without pulling his monitor leads off and pop my bra open at the same time, sidle him up to my breast, and then we are off on the magic carpet ride.

Happy New Year, sweet and precious boy. I am so glad you made it.

January 2

Does being a mother mean that your heart is cracked open forever?

This morning as I was feeding Tenzin, I noticed the nurses packing baby Christopher up to leave. I was interested because while I have been keeping my eye on Christopher, a delicate, quiet baby with seemingly no complications, I had never seen his mom. I figured that our schedules were just off, but this morning I realized it wasn't that at all. His mom left him here the day he was born.

The nurses packed all he had—a few diapers, a box of wipes, some bottles, and his little name card—while a foster mother waited in the hallway. I had seen her, the woman who was going to be Christopher's first love, on my way to the NICU. She was older, and looked tired and overwhelmed. She had a teenager with her, a boy, probably another foster child.

I could hardly stand it. Here I've been so worried about Tenzin and all he doesn't have. When I asked, Rose told me that Christopher's mother was a drug addict who had given birth here before. A discussion about birth control for drug-addicted women ensued, but I couldn't join in. I had to will myself to stay in my chair holding my baby, instead of getting on the phone to marshal resources for Christopher. Could we bring him home? Who did I know who wanted a baby? I was sure I could find a nice gay couple that would shower him with love.

But of course, I did nothing. There was nothing for me to do. Baby Christopher was bundled and handed to a complete stranger. I will never know if he ever laid eyes on the woman who made him, but I will always wonder.

RAINY DAY. I spent it cleaning my new room here at the hospital, finishing shower thank-you notes, and nursing Tenzin. Felt a bit melancholy. Something about the light, and being here in the city. Glen came with bags and bags of food to restock the cooler he set up for me. We sat on the little green sofa, looking out at the rain and eating tangerines.

January 5

I took a taxi from the hospital to get my toes painted, because I needed to get out of the hospital and return, just for a moment, to life as I once knew it. I put on my black pregnancy pants, battered denim shirt, and a little lip gloss, and left Glen sound asleep in the hospital bed with his head and feet up. The moment I stepped off the elevator and saw people in their everyday clothes, going about their lives, I started to feel out of sync. The world looked exactly as it did before, but I felt completely different. The dissonance made everything seem surreal. I kept telling myself that I have survived the act of bringing a child into the world and am in the process of surviving the fight to keep him alive. But there weren't any billboards up for that.

I showed up at the salon with my hospital bracelets, the plastic strips that verify that I actually do have a child in the NICU, around my wrist. Because babies are often abducted from hospitals, nurses in the NICU must match the numbers on my band to the ones on Tenzin's. If the numbers are not the same, or if I don't have a band at all, the nurses are required, no matter what I say or how loudly my baby is crying, to restrict my access. I hadn't paid much attention to them, but outside of the hospital they're pretty noticeable. Yelena spotted them right away and raised her eyebrows when I walked into the salon. I told her the baby's fine, just having a bit of trouble breathing.

When I finally got my feet into the hot water, I asked Raya why she didn't warn me. I had a smile on my face, but I was serious, too. Why didn't anybody tell me how much it was going to hurt? There were a few nodding heads, and then Raya said, I know, I know. It's awful. And I said, You know? Where were you, where was everybody, when I was talking all that natural-childbirth shit? Someone should have told me that I was out of my mind and that it was like getting a root canal without anesthetic.

After an hour and a half of being out, I started to miss the baby like crazy. My breasts were leaking through the pads in my bra, and I felt an overwhelming need to get back to the hospital. It lifted me out of the chair and out of the salon and into a taxi and back to the hospital. It didn't stop until I flashed my wristband at the nurse, walked through the door of the NICU, and saw with my own eyes that my baby was alive. Still breathing through a tube strapped to his face, but alive.

January 9

Went out for a walk today with Glen. When we got back to the hospital, the security guards had Tenzin's name but not mine on their chart. I flashed my hospital I.D. bracelets a few times, and tried to calmly explain the situation, you know, that the baby is sick and I am rooming in, but they refused to let me up.

I don't know exactly what happened, but Glen says I turned into some kind of Warrior Woman. I remember that when I realized they were serious and not planning to let me up, I felt a sharp surge of energy and also a preternatural calm. Everything got quiet and still. I wasn't sure how it would go down, but it occurred to me that if these guys didn't change their minds about letting me upstairs to see my baby, I couldn't guarantee their safety.

I think I told them that I didn't care what their chart said, my baby was upstairs and I was going to see him, but I remember that I made a sharp gesture with my hands. I remember that afterward they both stepped back and let us pass. I remember everything being quiet until the elevator door closed in front of us. Then Glen made a joke about me being a superhero. He said as we were walking toward the elevator all he could think was, *I'm with her.*

We were still laughing about it hours later, likening it to the Star Wars moment when the Storm Troopers stop Obi-Wan and demand his identification. Obi-Wan waves his hand over their faces and says, "You don't need to see my identification," and they magically parrot back to him, "We don't need your identification," and let him and Luke pass unmolested.

It's now official. The Force they're talking about? It's the cosmic version of motherhood.

January 13

He's been off oxygen for six hours, with the cannula still in place. Everyone keeps checking on him to see how he's doing and telling me we'll be going home soon. Rose told me today that they've done all they can do for him here. It's time for him to go home and live. She keeps saying in that singsongy voice, Mr. Tenzeen, you are going home, Mr. Tenzeen. And then she pinches his cheeks and smiles.

Glen and I spoke to Dr. Thompson, who is authorizing his release tomorrow barring any major sat dips. He stressed that Tenzin was probably going to be one-hundred-percent fine, able to do everything a kid who hadn't had MAS could do. The difficulty, he said, would be his parents treating him like a sick kid all his life. That's the tendency, he said. Mothers and fathers, but mostly mothers, fretting over kids who have been sick, telling them they shouldn't do this and shouldn't do that, and projecting weak, sick child ideas all over them.

They were speaking in guyese about overprotective mothers, smothers. I was about to get pissed and vehemently deny that I would ever be that way, but then I thought I heard Tenzin's monitor beeping and ran over to make sure he was okay. Clearly, I've got to take baby steps.

The biggest news is that the baby is going to sleep with me tonight! I can't believe it. The moment we've all been waiting for. After dinner, if he makes it without the cannula for three hours, one of the nurses is going to wheel him into my room and we get to be there together for the entire night. No tubes, no machines, no constant in-and-out of doctors and other parents. Just us: my boy and me, in the quiet dark.

January 14

It was hard to say goodbye to everybody, but easy to leave the hospital. I hugged and thanked all the nurses I could find. I accepted and read the card wishing Tenzin a happy and successful life, signed by all of the doctors. I collected all fourteen bottles of my breast milk from the refrigerator and put them in a cooler bought expressly, no pun intended, for this purpose.

Angie wheeled us downstairs as Glen pulled up in the big car we bought for just this moment. After much wrestling with straps, I settled Tenzin in his new seat.

Within seconds we were on the freeway and the hospital was far behind us. Glen put his hand over mine and I felt the warmth of it, of him, radiate through my whole body. I thought about how Glen had showed up for me and we had showed up for Tenzin. And I thought that really, when it comes down to it, that's what life is all about: showing up for the people you love, again and again, until you can't show up anymore.

I put my hand over his and said, We did it. We made a baby and now we are taking him home.

Glen looked at me and said, Yep. I think that about covers it.

And then we laughed.

Nine

LIKE EVERY OTHER warm-blooded woman of childbearing age, I worried a great deal about the many wonderful experiences I would have to forgo once I had a baby. Along with sleep, travel, and ready-to-wear, movies were at the top of my list of things I simply could not imagine life without. New and old, foreign and domestic, comedies, dramas, and documentaries: I watched them tucked cozily into bed at night, or lounging on the sofa in the early morning. They were like chocolate to me: delicious, transporting, and essential.

Now I can't believe I watched so many movies. When I go down the list of films on Netflix, I am appalled by how hard it is to find one I haven't seen. How many hours of my life have I spent on long, artfully drawn journeys into other people's lives? Human beings crave narrative because we glimpse the universal through the specific and feel less alone. But I feel nothing but relief to be so fully occupied living my own life that I am no longer compelled to watch other people living theirs.

Call me a snob, but where I used to find the infinite ways people resolve their endlessly complicated lives fascinating, I now see a bunch of stylized variations on a theme. It's not that storytelling or art itself isn't valuable, because it irrefutably is. I couldn't bring myself to write this book if it wasn't. I am just newly aware that it may not be *absolutely necessary.* I can have a perfectly fulfilling life, without entering the mind-streams of dozens of artists trying to make sense of their temporal existence. This feels blasphemous to think, let alone write, but I have to be brutally honest here, because that's my job.

I had a baby and yes, I am like every new mother in that all I want to do is stare at him all day. But beneath that desire is a more profound truth: *He* is the story! The fact that he's here, that he's mine, and that anything could happen to either of us. The incontrovertible truth that he materialized miraculously: a flesh-and-blood manifestation of a figment of my imagination, and that I have to work like hell to subject him to all of the yummy and none of the yucky stuff of my own childhood.

In this new live-it-or-leave-it modality, I realize I may be flirting dangerously with myopia, and that it could be a stage, like teething, that will pass. I may wake up one morning rabid for a trip to the multiplex, but I don't think so. The transition from observer to participant has been inexplicably liberating. It's the how-to-live-your-own-life version of learning to swim: Once you know how, you no longer need lessons. You just get in the ocean and go.

This, I'll call it "life competence" for lack of a better term, is permeating my life. Now when I am lusting after a pair of boots, I have to ask myself if I'll be wearing those to the decidedly unglamorous supermarket down the street to pick up diapers and sliced turkey, and whether or not the toe will be a help or a hindrance when it's time to unfold the stroller. When I consider yet another price tag, for anything, I am forced to consider how much interest the same amount of money would earn in a 529 college savings plan.

I can't say that I am completely sober, but the whole process, that holy trinity of hunt, acquisition, and display, is breaking down as my concern shifts from looking great and feeling slightly alienated to feeling incredible and looking relatively well-put-together. Instead of talking through "stuff," I am talking to my son. I am not saying a girl can't have it all, because I am all for making life expand to meet your limitless vision, but I am saying that, first, said girl has to know what "all" really is.

My work habits have also taken a turn. A few days ago, a friend with writer's block asked about my favorite places to write. Was it the desert or the forest, a spa or hotel, a lonely retreat cabin or a convivial writers' colony? Struck by the question, I flashed on all the climates and landscapes I have pursued in the name of writing, all the rooms and houses, offices and shacks I've spent months and years trying to transform into the perfect writing space. Where did it get me? Where is my bookshelf filled with titles?

I didn't want to shatter the hopeful promise of the room of one's own, that mystical and magical place the muse will be unable to resist, but again, I had to tell the truth.

My bed, I said. My dining-room table, the tiny thirty-dollar desk on casters I bought at IKEA, the sofa. At the moment, I am writing at the kitchen table. Tenzin is strapped into his carrot-encrusted high chair on my right, engrossed in picking up star-shaped banana puffs. Every five minutes, he makes a high-pitched yelp to get my attention, and I reach for a new thrill to keep him occupied, but by the end of the day I will have written five hundred words over my thousand-word allotment. As an extra bonus, I get to sneak a quick kiss or neck nuzzle in between graphs.

My friend was taken aback, but not after I explained that writing-room obsession had claimed many years of actual writing time; that the cultivation of the perfect space was my procrastination activity of choice. I told her that back when I was searching for the perfect space, I'd be lucky if I even turned on my computer, let alone banged out a few lines. I probably will never catch up to Stephen King, who at a professed eighty to eighty-five pages a day makes me sick with envy, but now I am closer than ever to writing a book a year, and I owe it all to Tenzin.

Of course, it's not all chocolate and roses over here. Yesterday I heard from one of my cousins that he has replaced me in my mother's will. I can only assume that her response to my request for an apology is to disinherit me. It hurts, but she's been talking for so many years about how she doesn't believe in leaving anything to one's children, I am numb to it. Of course, now that I have a child and can't watch the evening news without wondering how on earth any of us are going to survive, I can't imagine not wanting to take care of my children and my children's children.

I also got a call from the caretaker of the little house in Mendocino I spent so much time transforming. He told me that my mother told him to throw all of my clothes and belongings away. *Todo,* he said. *¡En la basura!* The truth is that what my mother is doing hurts so much I can no longer feel it, but I am more confident than ever about my decision to keep my distance. It's not just me now getting yanked about by her anger and ambivalence, her refusal to acknowledge my right to my own story, it's Tenzin, too. All these years I haven't been able to stand up for myself, but now, for him, I'm willing to walk through fire. Which is about what becoming a mother without a mother feels like.

There are other complications, too. Like all the things I miss— sleep, for example. When people told me to rest while I was pregnant, I didn't know what to think. I'm an eight-hour-a-night person, and I figured I might have to settle for six. Not two to four, interrupted every forty-five minutes by piercing screams, hurried bottle preparation, and hushed whispers to a disoriented creature in a padded box. Not so little sleep that I would be rendered virtually incompetent physically, emotionally, and in tens of other ways I am too tired to remember.

I miss being able to wander aimlessly, not knowing the time, not caring, not having to phone home to make sure baby boy isn't having a ballistic fit. Being "responsible" for my time is undeniably a mark of my growing appreciation for its value, but God damn, it's hell. These days, if I am on my own I am either on the clock paying by the hour, or feeling guiltily beholden to my wonderful but sometimes overwhelmed partner who has his own work to do. Naptime, no matter how much I want to believe is free time, is not. I can't go out of earshot, and must be ready to stop whatever I am doing to attend to the babe. Gone are my two-hour mini-vacations in the bathtub.

I miss my breasts, which, while still perfectly lovely and functional, have definitely gone through some changes since performing their duties as organic milk dispensers. I miss my flat stomach. It's coming back slowly, but I have the sinking suspicion it will never be the same. I miss having what felt like an endless supply of mental and emotional stamina. Where I used to seek out conversation, licking my lips at the possibility of a "meaningful exchange,"

I am increasingly more selective about how I expend my precious energy.

And even though loving another human being a thousand times more than you love yourself is arguably the most subversive thrill left in this object-obsessed, hypercapitalist world, I miss having only myself to worry about. The constant fear for my baby's psychological and physical well-being is noble, but enervating in every way.

Even so, as I consider the fact that I, once terrified of spiders, will now reach into my son's crib to kill one with my bare hands, I am struck by the human ability—propensity, even—for regeneration and change. It's true that we are what we think, but the caveat is that what we think changes, and thank goodness. If we weren't gradually disabused of limited ideas about the world and ourselves, who would we be? Five years ago I thought I could find marital bliss with an unfaithful musician, and happiness in a house renovation. Ten years ago, I thought meat was murder and meat eaters should be forced to raise and slaughter their own suppers. Thirteen years ago, I thought I was going to marry a devout Muslim and raise ten kids on a tiny island with no running water or electricity.

That we can change our minds is the easy part, it's figuring out what to change them to that is nearly impossible. I suggest an identity, or should I say a series of decisions, that make one happy and ensure the psychological well-being of the next generation. Isn't that the ultimate freedom? To know you're serving yourself and the present while at the same time taking care of the future?

I am a mother and a partner now. After all those years of wanting, denying, and being afraid, I stopped searching and embraced what was right in front of me. It's hard, this making a healthy family, probably the hardest work I've ever done. But every day, when

I look at this little being I have the extreme good fortune to call my son, I thank the part of me that had the wherewithal, despite all the doubt and fear, to go ahead and embrace motherhood, to get on the ride and let it take me away.

I have no regrets.

ACKNOWLEDGMENTS

Everyone needs a team, and I feel blessed to have one so loyal and devoted.

Thanks to my literary agent, Jennifer Rudolph Walsh, for being one of the toughest, smartest women I've ever known and for having my back. Thanks to Geoff Kloske and Sarah McGrath for leading the Riverhead charge with insight and grace, and for making this a better book. Thanks to Amy Hertz and Cindy Spiegel, who have moved on but are not forgotten. Thanks, again, to Susan Petersen Kennedy.

Thanks to Barbara Wilson and Alba Camarena for making sure I fund my Roth IRA. Thanks to Aurélie Moulin for keeping my virtual world beautiful and up-to-date. Thanks to Ekajati Moore for orchestrating my day-to-day with élan. Thanks to all of the lecture agents for keeping me comfortable on the road.

Thanks to my father, for always trying to find integrity no

matter how difficult the circumstances. Thanks to my mother for having the courage to live her truth and, by example, teaching me to live mine. Thanks to Randall and Nicole for being there through it all.

Finally, thanks to all the readers who find meaning in my work. You make it all worthwhile.

ABOUT THE AUTHOR

Rebecca Walker has received numerous awards and accolades for her writing and her activism. Her memoir *Black, White, and Jewish* was a national bestseller, and her work has appeared in many anthologies and other publications. Her feminist anthology *To Be Real,* in print for more than ten years, has become a standard text in women's studies courses across the country. Walker lives in Hawaii.